inspired to pray

"Phil Pringle is one of the most influential leaders of our time. He has a burning passion and zeal for the lost and hurting. This book will change your view on prayer and how to communicate with God and will bless you in amazing ways!"
—*Pastor Matthew Barnett*
  Senior Pastor, Dream Center, Los Angeles, California

"Phil Pringle is a dynamic teacher who is constantly challenging those around him to pursue something greater than themselves. In *Inspired to Pray*, he perfectly illustrates the incredible dynamic of prayer—that it is a relational conversation with the God of the universe. With biblically sound teaching and creativity, *Inspired to Pray* will give you a strong foundation to live a life founded and rooted in prayer."
—*John Bevere*
  Bestselling Author and Speaker
  Cofounder, Messenger International, Colorado Springs, Colorado

"Dr. Pringle is a great writer, and he is also a wonderful artist. In *Inspired to Pray*, he has combined both of these gifts to create a great work of literature and art. This book is the best of two worlds, and it discusses every possible subject connected with prayer in a most artistic manner. You will be able to view prayer in a new dimension."
—*Dr. David Yonggi Cho*
  Chairman, Church Growth International, Seoul, Korea

"Through this book you have the opportunity to glean some wisdom and insights from Phil Pringle's life and journey. I heartily recommend it!"
—*Mark Conner*
  Senior Minister, CityLife Church, Melbourne, Australia

"*Inspired to Pray* is a walk with Phil Pringle in an up close and personal way that will inspire, teach and warm your heart. You will feel the heartbeat of an artist painting pictures on your heart with his prayer insights. Genius of an idea!"
—*Dr. Frank Damazio*
  Senior Pastor, City Bible Church, Portland, Oregon

"*Inspired to Pray* is a much-needed prod to remind us of the call to come before the Almighty God in prayer. Through his enthralling creativeness and authenticity, Phil Pringle lays down many amazing principles and truths apropos of prayer in this masterpiece."
—*Kong Hee*
  Senior Pastor, City Harvest Church, Singapore

"Comprehensive and compelling."
—*Bill Hybels*
  Senior Pastor, Willow Creek Community Church
  South Barrington, Illinois

"God has the perfect answer for us in every situation if we sill simply ask Him! These times of unusual challenges call for renewed hope in Christ. Pastor Phil Pringle's *Inspired to Pray* paints a lyrical picture of how our lives can be dramatically transformed if we will only pray to God and trust that He has great plans for us!"
—*Bishop T.D. Jakes, Sr.*
  The Potter's House of Dallas, Texas

"For people wanting wisdom in a world of conflicting messages."
—*John C. Maxwell*
  Bestselling Author

"Phil Pringle has a fresh, unique way of looking at everything, and there is a strong anointing on his life and ministry. He writes from a wealth of knowledge and experience."
—*Rick Shelton*
  Senior Minister, Life Christian Center, St. Louis, Missouri

"*Inspired to Pray* is an eloquent and much-needed reminder that there is nothing we cannot rise above as long as we keep the path of communication flowing between ourselves and God. As Phil Pringle so beautifully demonstrates in this unique and lyrical book, one of the most empowering ways to abide in God's will is through prayer."
—*Kenneth Ulmer*
  Senior Pastor, Faithful Central Bible Church, Los Angeles, California

"Crammed full of extraordinary insights . . . I highly recommend it."
—*C. Peter Wagner*
  Wagner Leadership Institute, Colorado Springs, Colorado

inspired to pray

[the art of seeking God]

Phil Pringle

Regal

From Gospel Light
Ventura, California, U.S.A.

Regal

Published by Regal
From Gospel Light
Ventura, California, U.S.A.
www.regalbooks.com
Printed in the U.S.A.

Internal layout by Velvet Creative (www.velvet.com.au)
Cover painting: "Prayer" by Phil Pringle (www.philpringlegallery.com)
All poems and paintings by Phil Pringle

Previously published as *If? The Art of Prayer* by PaX Ministries Pty Ltd. ABN 97 003 162 392
Locked Bag No. 8, Dee Why, 2099, Australia, Tel: +61 2 9972 8688 Fax: +61 2 9972 8640,
www.ccc.org.au/pax. Printed by Hyde Park Press.

1   2   3   4   5   6   7   8   9   /   15   14   13   12   11   10   09

contents

about the author

Phil Pringle is the founding and senior pastor of one of Australia's fastest growing, largest, most exciting churches. In 1980, Phil and his wife, Chris, arrived in Sydney, Australia from New Zealand, armed with faith and a vision to build a dynamic church that would grow and impact a city and a nation for Christ.

A frequent guest on TV programs hosted by noted Christian leaders such as Joyce Meyer, Benny Hinn, T.D. Jakes and many others around the world, Phil has seen powerful moves of God break out, the glory of the Lord engulf the atmosphere, and people touched and permanently changed by the Holy Spirit. He has overseen the planting of new churches in major cities throughout the world. Today, there are more than 200 C3 churches, which collectively make up Christian City Church International around the globe ("C3i").

Christian City Church ("C3" Oxford Falls) reflects Phil's passion to energize cities and nations by every available, relevant means. During the past 25 years, he has overseen this vibrant church, which has grown to nearly 5,000 members, as well as more than 200 new C3 church plants around the world. In addition to its stimulating teaching ministry, C3 has an internationally renowned accredited education program, including kindergarten through high school, and offers four-year college degrees in several disciplines. C3 also operates **TV studio CCTV**, which creates professional-quality broadcast programming, and **ccworships**, a record label that produces and distributes original and contemporary praise and worship music worldwide, originating from C3's own Oxford Falls congregation. (Visit **www.ccceshop.com.au** for details.)

Phil is the author of several top-selling books, including *Faith, Keys to Financial Excellence, Healing the Wounded Spirit, Top 10 Qualities of a Great Leader* (titled *Leadership Excellence* in the U.S.) and *Dead for Nothing?* (featured on *This Is Your Day* with Benny Hinn and on *Enjoying Everyday Life* with Joyce Meyer). His latest book, *But God*, is a colorful reminder that we may go through the worst of storms in life, *but God* always rescues His faithful ones!

For information on Phil Pringle's preaching podcasts, email messages ("Leadership Files") and itinerary, and for details about Christian City Church service times and conferences, visit **www.ccc.org.au**.

introduction

One reason I wrote this book is so you will begin to pray; or, if you pray already, that your prayer life might be enriched and that you will become inspired to an increase in prayer. My hope—my *prayer*—is that you will pray not just in moments now and then, but every day throughout your life, not merely saying something while you are doing something else, but that you will stop each day just to pray, giving the effort enough time for you to disconnect with the busyness of your world and to more deeply connect with Jesus.

Prayer dies so easily within us and in the church nowadays. What a blessing it would be for this book to affect churches and to impact groups and families to be inspired to increased prayer. However, prayer simply cannot revive in the church unless prayer first revives in her leaders. That brings me to the other reason I wrote this book: So that those with any level of influence—leaders, pastors, ministers—will gather people to pray and to encourage people to create room in their schedules and on their calendars in order to make prayer a priority. Real prayer, deep and meaningful prayer, where they all pray together to the Lord.

> *"Spiritual growth is impossible apart from the practice of prayer."* [1]
> —Kenneth Boa

Prayer, much more than just muttering religious words, enjoys connecting with the God of heaven Himself. John 4:24 says that God is a Spirit. We too are spirit as much as we are flesh. This flesh will pass away, but our spirit will not. That eternal part of us continues forever, and connects in worship with God. Our minds fail to bridge the gap between earth and heaven; but prayer releases our spirit into communion with God in another world: *His* world. Our body registers the impact of God with us, but our body is not the root of that bond. When we pray, the deepest part of who we are in our core, in our spirit, connects with the eternal God.

Prayer is the womb in which we give birth to things yet unseen. Prayer is the site where we "build" our life first in the invisible world. Prayer is the field of war where we command the authority given to us from God, unlocking forces more powerful than any that may rise against us.

God will reconnect this world to Himself, not through science, government or technology, but through people—people of prayer. We look for better methods. God looks for better people. **What** we do is

either powerful or not, because **we** are either powerful or not. It's not the method that contains power; it's the people. We tend to think that the force of our own knowledge will fetch the solutions we need, when in actuality answers are only found through the prayer of an awakened spirit.

Dr. David Cho of Seoul, South Korea, reveals that the secret of his success in pastoring the largest church in the world is *prayer*: "Prayer is the key to revival. Prayer is the key to your success. Prayer is the key to personal victory. I ask you to pray. I ask you to pray. I ask you a third time to pray. Prayer is the foundation of the Kingdom of God. Only through prayer can we carry out God's command in our lives." [2]

Edward Bounds, famous for prayer, declared: "God shapes the world by prayer. Prayers are deathless. The lips that uttered them may be closed in death, the heart that felt them may have ceased to beat, but the prayers live before God, and God's heart is set on them and prayers outlive the lives of those who uttered them; outlive a generation, outlive an age, outlive a world." [3]

William Penn said of George Fox: "But above all he excelled in prayer. The inwardness and weight of his spirit, the reverence and solemnity of his address and behavior, and the fewness and fullness of his words have often struck even strangers with admiration as they used to reach others with consolation. The most awful, living, reverend frame I ever felt or beheld, I must say, was his prayer. And truly it was a testimony. He knew and lived nearer to the Lord than other men, for they that know him most will see most reason to approach him with reverence and fear." [4]

Kathryn Kuhlman, the extraordinary healing evangelist of the 20th century, is reported to have said, "The greatest power that God has given to any individual is the power of prayer."

Gordon Lindsay, who was recognized as a major contributor to the healing revivals of the 1940s and '50s, said: "Prayer must become as natural as breathing. With such prayer, men defeat spiritual powers arrayed against them that no human means could overcome." [5]

Charles Spurgeon, often referred to as the Prince of Preachers, who was Pastor of the London Metropolitan Tabernacle, the largest church of its time, said: "Whether we like it or not, asking is the rule of the Kingdom." [6] He pointed out that the enormous success of his church and ministry was due to the continual prayer of four hundred intercessors praying day and night in the basement beneath his church.

It is commonly recognized that most of the Missions movements that began throughout the world were birthed from a prayer meeting lasting around one hundred years under the leadership of Count Von Zinzendorf of Moravia. John and Charles Wesley were also impacted by people from that prayer meeting. Their lives in turn changed the history of the United Kingdom and beyond. [7]

I recently heard a speaker referring to the unique qualities of each people group around the world and their contribution to the Kingdom of God. He spoke of how the Americans brought organization and buildings, the South Americans brought family values, the Australians and New Zealanders brought worship, and the Asians brought prayer. This was an interesting observation and may relate in some ways to current emphases around the world, but in no way can we say that one culture is more "given" to prayer than another. Prayer is not the culture of a particular people group, but of the Kingdom of God. All believers are called to prayer. It's not a gift for certain people, but for every believer and every church.

> "Prayer is not a special gift some believers have and others do not.
> It is the practice of every believer."
> —Frank Damazio

Prayer is not an optional extra. Prayers are the lungs of the Spirit. Just as surely as our body would die without breathing, our spirit would wither without prayer. The church breathes through prayer. Every living thing breathes. If we don't breathe, we die. So does the church. So does any believer.

We are called to bring the atmosphere of another world to this planet—the atmosphere of heaven. This is only possible if we are breathing the air of that place. The air of prayer.

The greatest spiritual awakenings of history have been born of prayer, no matter what continent on earth. The church herself was born in a prayer meeting in the Middle East. The great "Third Awakening" in America began in downtown Manhattan in a Dutch Reform church with six businessmen, under the guidance of a layman named Jeremiah Lanphier. Within six months there were ten thousand people gathering at these noon prayer meetings in major cities throughout America. The prayer meetings spread to Ireland and Wales, then to the United Kingdom, and to the rest of the world. The Germans birthed the Moravian prayer meeting, which was responsible for spiritual renewal throughout the world. [8]

Prayer is universal. No one group, either currently or down throughout history, can be attributed as the sole and natural possessors of this unique bridge with God. Every church and every believer must learn the lifestyle of prayer. Not even the Apostles had a lock on prayer. Matthew 26:40 says that

Jesus was shocked when his own disciples couldn't even sustain one hour of prayer. Yet it is prayer that provides the foundation of success for the church. When Jesus told the disciples to wait in Jerusalem, they didn't just wander around the city. They gathered in the upper room and continued in one accord in prayer until the Spirit fell upon them (see Acts 1:14).

In Matthew 21:12, one of the first things Jesus did was to cleanse the temple of everything that was obscuring the fact that it was a House of prayer. We fill our services with everything but prayer of the kind where everyone prays. Even when we do have times of prayer, it is generally one person at the front saying a prayer on their own while everyone remains silent, ending their prayer with a corporate "Amen."

We must bring the prayer meeting out of the back room and into mainstream church services so all of us can engage in prayer just as we sing together songs of worship. Prayer is the church at work. It is the church breathing. It is the church exercising her authority together. It is the backbone of the church's walk with God. It is the bridge that keeps us connected to Him.

We don't have to always be praying for something. Prayer in itself is enough to simply commune with God. We need to recover times when we seek God simply for Himself, rather than going to Him only for what He can do for us. We need to seek Him because we thirst for Him, and not just because He might do something on our behalf. We may not be money changing like the traders in the temple, but we do need to rid the temple of things that stand in the way of the church being a House of prayer for all nations.

notes

1. Kenneth Boa, *Handbook to Prayer: Praying Scripture Back to God* (Atlanta, GA: Trinity House, 1997).
2. Dr. David Yonggi Cho, *Church Growth Manual 4* (Seoul, Korea: Church Growth International, 1992), p. 49.
3. Edward M. Bounds, *Power Through Prayer* (Oak Harbor, WA, Logos Research Systems, Inc. 1999).
4. See http://www.strecorsoc.org/gfox/wmpenn.html.
5. Gordon Lindsay, *Prayer That Moves Mountains* (Dallas, TX: Christ for the Nations, 1988).
6. See http://www.weeks-g.dircon.co.uk/quotes_p.htm & http://mysite.verizon.net/vzenuft3/letters/id121.html.
7. *McClintock and Strong Encyclopedia*, electronic database. Copyright © 2000, 2003 by Biblesoft, Inc. All rights reserved.
8. Ibid.

If My people who are **called by My name**
will humble themselves,
and PRAY and *seek* My face, and turn from their
wicked ways,
then I will *hear from heaven,*
and WILL forgive their sin and heal their land.
—*2 Chronicles 7:14*

if my people

Where are they?
Who is there?
Has felt the cry to breathe again,
Air from another world,
They breathe this wind with voice from there,
"He sounds like no other."
They rush to hear the sound of the people of "If,"
Who heard "If," and said "we will,"
Deep into the dark night,
Their prayers pierced through the noise,
Of an earth mad with anger.

Broken HEARTED they cry for others,
As though it was themselves,
But their highest cry is for His face,
And seeking they find,
Emerging glowing,
Different, calm, unassailable,
The faces of lions, kings even!
This secret place discovered by the tribe of "If,"
Them who said "Yes," and did.
Their land heals, their walk is strong.
They wear the face of Eternal's realm.
This "If" people.

*T*he pivotal word defining our call is "if." Nearly every response from heaven hinges on this tiny conjunction. All the possibilities of all of our lives hang on "if." This Scripture is saying that God will heal our nations entirely IF we will humble ourselves and pray.

It's an astonishing insight that God's own people are so disconnected from Him that they have to be commanded to pray. One would think that if we are His people, we would be communicating with Him on a regular basis. Yet, He calls us to pray, promising that "if" we do, then there will be answers. The most natural thing for believers is to pray. Yet, it is also too easily smothered. Revival is God's people praying again.

Pride increases when prayer decreases. Prayer acknowledges that we are insufficient in ourselves. We need God and we need to pray.

"And seek My face…"

God's face is discovered in prayer. We have no relationship with God without prayer.

"And turn…"

The power to turn from evil is found in prayer. Without prayer we are powerless. Evil gains ground in the prayerless soul. In prayer we find desire and strength to destroy sin's power over us. We can be told that sin's power is broken over us, but this victory really only materializes in prayer. It's the difference between knowing of the work of the cross and experiencing it.

If our spiritual life is strong, then we are empowered to do what God wants. The ability to surrender, the capacity to do the will of God, requires the fuel of the Spirit, which fills us as we pray.

This is not the prayer of a single person. It is the prayer of a people. "If" we get ourselves together in prayer, united for the same purpose, then we unleash the greatest power of the Kingdom. Entire nations will be healed in these days through the power of humble, united prayer from the gathered church.

God has promised that our nations will be delivered, restored, favored and healed if we, the people of God in all the nations of the world, will call upon Him.

All that's required is IF!

NOW this is the CONFIDENCE that we have in Him,
that IF we ask anything according to His will, HE HEARS US.
And IF we know that He hears us, WHATEVER WE ASK,
we know that WE HAVE THE PETITIONS THAT WE
HAVE ASKED of Him.

—*1 John 5:14-15*

confidence

The will of God, clear as the sun,
Lost found, sick healed,
The dead alive again
Living life for God,
IF you pray for this you have His ear,
You have His answers,
Unhindered assurance,
A witness box of jurors within
Hammer yes and Amen.

There is also an assurance within our soul that God has heard us. And if God hears us, then our prayers are answered.

We can enjoy being confident that anything we pray for along these lines will be answered.

Confidence in prayer is at a premium. There is little power in an anxious prayer.

God hears prayers that echo His purposes. He is deaf to prayers opposing His will. We know He hears us through what His Word tells us. He watches over His Word to perform it (see Jeremiah 1:12)! When His Word fills our prayers and we declare His promises, His Spirit releases power to fulfill them.

The word "whatsoever" reappears time and again when we are invited to pray. God's will is to answer our prayers and to fulfill our dreams. He simply needs to know them. That's why we need to pray them.

IF *anyone*
sees his brother sinning a sin . . .
HE WILL ASK...
and He [G O D] will *give* him *life*.
—*1 John 5:16*

mercy

Too easy to judge,
Too hard to pray,
But, IF with mercy and embarrassed spirit we cry for another,
God hears our love,
Not reserved for priests,
This gap waits for **anyone**,
You, me, unjudging,
Praying, asking, pleading,
The promise of mercy afloat in heaven alights on a sinner's soul,
Because you saw, you prayed, you asked for them.

The Kingdom of God runs on incredibly powerful laws. One of which is intercession; that is, standing before God on behalf of another. All of us can do this. It's the "power of attorney." Another person fighting for us will usually argue our case more powerfully than we do ourselves.

There are hundreds of instances of intercession throughout Scripture. Abraham interceded for Sodom and Gomorrah, hoping to rescue his nephew Lot from the judgment against those cities (see Genesis 18). Moses often interceded for

the Israelites that God would not destroy them when they complained against Him. Jesus Himself interceded for His disciples that they would be united in John 17. Paul interceded for all the Christians and churches he was responsible for (see Ephesians 4:13). Epaphras, Paul's disciple, interceded for the Colossian believers (see Colossians 1:7).

In 1 John 5:16, John is telling us that when we see other Christians doing wrong, we are to pray for them—not judge them, gossip about them, or write letters to them—but pray for them. We are promised that IF we do this, God will give them life.

IF you
ask
anything
in **MY NAME,**
I will
DO it.

—*John 14:14*

anything

His unblemished name,
Weight enough to change history,
Weight that crushes hell, opens heaven, invokes God,
This Most High, holy name,
So freely given,
IF we would but ask
In that name,
Anything can—no, will—be done!

In Acts 19:13-16, the seven sons of Sceva fashioned themselves as exorcists. Upon trying to cast out a demon, the spirit responded to them, "Jesus I know, and Paul I know; but who are you?" They did not know Christ, and they were completely overpowered by the demon, who stripped them of all their clothes, and they fled.

Jesus offers us the opportunity to ask for anything—which literally means "anything." The qualifier is that this "anything" must be asked for in the name of Jesus. This means that our prayers must be aligned with His character, His nature, and His purposes. When we are in this kind of harmony with God, the promise that He has declared it means that He will do it.

The name of Jesus encompasses all the nature, character, and purposes of God. It is also the seal of our authority in the earth. Even demons know the name of Jesus.

However, the name is powerful in Person, not just as some magic charm. To ask in the name of another is to ask "on behalf of." We are representing the purposes of God on earth. Whatever we ask in His name needs to further God's purpose for us or for others. Thus, we cannot pray for things such as people being killed—that's the purpose of the devil, to kill, steal and destroy (see John 10:10). Thus, it is evident that we need to know the Owner of the name Jesus before we are effective in using it.

5)

IF you **abide** in
Me, and
My words **ABIDE** in you,
you will ask what you *desire,*
and it
shall be **done for you**.
BY THIS My **Father** is **GLORIFIED**,
that you *bear much fruit*;
so you will be
My disciples.
—John 15:7-8

abide

O so many things we ache for,
Some right, some wrong,
But He is high above them all.
We abide because we ache for Him.
So IF He is our desire,
He is our home,
Our life.
So fruit forms to the side.
Much fruit,
Intake greater than outflow,
Our cup overflows.
The disciple abides
Living above grapplings of this place,
Disciplines binding him close,
Unbroken communion reflecting glory
To Him.

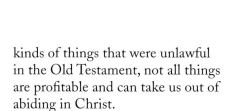

The power of prayer is in God hearing His word echoed in heaven from earth. When His Word abides in us, our thinking aligns with His.

Abiding in Jesus is communing continually with him, living in a way that we avoid removing Him from that place. Even though in the New Testament we are set free to do all kinds of things that were unlawful in the Old Testament, not all things are profitable and can take us out of abiding in Christ.

It is a spirit of continual prayer of fellowship that keeps us abiding in Christ. So when we are in Him and His Word is in us, we will pray extremely effectively. Our prayers will be answered. This bearing of fruit glorifies God and proves us to be His disciples.

If **ANY**
of you **lacks wisdom**, let him
ask of **GOD**,
who gives
to all *liberally*
and without reproach,
and it **will** be given to him.
—*James 1:5*

wisdom

Sweet sister, befriend me often,
Lady wisdom my love,
Defeat my lust, my raging flesh,
Back down quick tongue,
Retreat angered soul,
Awake lazy soul,
Heed this beautiful one,
This ever desirable mate.
Court her before all others,
Seek her at the head,
IF you do this, all other prayers,
All dreams and aches will be shaped by her.
The eunuch clothes Esther,
She assures favor with the king.
Seek her, she will come,
She will clothe you.

"*I* don't know how I'm going to do this. I don't know what to do with my job, my children, my family, how to get out of this financial problem, how to help these people for Christ..."

Many people deal with these kinds of struggles; it's not uncommon to not know what to do. But it's amazing how infrequently we ask God for the wisdom to "do" life. We read books, get counsel, go to seminars, think deeply, ask friends, and yet God has perfect wisdom for us in every situation, if we will simply ask Him.

Sometimes we are asking God to do what we are meant to be doing. All we need is the wisdom to know what to do. Our greatest need is wisdom.

...nothing you could wish for holds a candle to her.
—Proverbs 3:15 (*THE MESSAGE*)

God declares that He will give us power to get wealth (see Deuteronomy 8:18). He would rather give us this power to create wealth than to just give wealth itself to us. He wants to show us how to do the task, rather than just giving us what we can already do for ourselves. We are praying for a vase when God wants to give us clay. We are meant to be involved in the creative process. Creativity is not just about art, sculpture, music, or dance. Creativity is the inventor and engineer harnessing the laws of aerodynamics that enable us to fly higher than any bird.

James reveals that God gives wisdom without reproach. Beautiful! We are to approach God without hesitation, not nervous of rebuke. God doesn't take the attitude, "All right, I'll give it to you, but you remember: I'll be watching!"

Some people take advantage of the fact that they are giving us something, in order to correct us about all sorts of things in our life. Not so with God—far the contrary. It's His pleasure to give liberally to His obedient children. Whatever we ask for, He will give with overflowing abundance.

...it is your Father's good pleasure to give you the kingdom.
—Luke 12:32

BUT

let him ask in **FAITH**,

with **NO DOUBTING**,

for he who d o u b t s is like a *wave of the sea*
d r i v e n and *tossed* by the wind.

For **LET NOT THAT MAN SUPPOSE THAT HE
WILL RECEIVE ANYTHING FROM THE LORD;**
he is a *double-minded* man,
UNSTABLE in all his ways.

—*James 1:6-8*

no doubt

Shall I?
Shan't I?
"I will,"
"I won't,"
The second guess,
The dark aftermath of bold decisions,
The grinding teeth of an unwitting word,
The tossing of the double-minded man,
Restless soul,
Make up your unmade mind,
Tottering on reason's edge,
Weak at the knees,
This Thomas IF is the wrong "if,"
Sad, he needs, but doesn't receive
It's faith Yahweh says "Yes" to,

Leave your fake piety,
Be bold, stop crawling cringing,
Thinking this is prayer.
Be bold, stand, stand and stand,
Mind unshifted, steady and calm,
Receiving everything offered from heaven.

*J*ames tells us to pray with a fully convinced mind; in other words, not to be double-minded (in the Greek, *dipsuchos*[1]) or "two-souled." Confused desires make a confused mind. In this place, we receive nothing from the Lord. A double mind is an "unmade" mind; whereas a decisive mind is a mind "made up." When we hesitate, second-guess, and look backwards, we reinforce "double-mindedness." This opposes faith, which is singleness of mind. This is where we have burnt our bridges behind us, closed our options to the left and right, and have become committed to that one thing we are pursuing.

The double-minded person falls easy prey to trouble and is easily tossed by any blowing wind—good or bad. We are better off to make a decision even if wrong, rather than to make none at all. Once we are moving, taking steps, God will guide us.

Without steps we are motionless. In this state we can't be guided. We are guided as we step out, not before. Faith steps out. Abraham stepped out, not knowing where he was going, but simply knowing that God had a destination for him and that he would receive direction as he began moving.

The double-minded person has a lifestyle that is unstable in every area, and therefore receives nothing from the Lord. The opposite is true for the faith-minded person, one who is committed and decisive. They are stable in all their ways and receive everything from the Lord.

note
1.   James Strong, *Strong's Concordance* (Nashville, TN: Thomas Nelson, 1984), Greek word #1374.

8

IF you

then, being evil,

know how to

GIVE GOOD GIFTS

to your c h i l d r e n ,

HOW MUCH MORE

will your Father

who is in heaven

GIVE GOOD THINGS

to those who ASK Him!

—Matthew 7:11

good things

How warm a father's embrace.
How kind his words,
Soft, even healing, not rejecting,
Seeking to give good,
The much, the best.
It's His glory that you're blessed,
Not that you're not.
IF we do not ask,
"how much more" tarries.
If we ask, He rejoices to pour out.
Ten thousand times a day would not be enough,
To render unending praise
To a father eternal in blessing.

*G*od knows how to give good gifts to His children. It's also true that He wants to. If I was known to pray for my children to be poor, fail at everything, become diseased and sickly, live broken down lives with broken down provisions, anyone could rightly judge me to be an evil father. Yet, many believe this is God's intention toward us! Unbelievable. It is blasphemy to charge Him with this. It is the devil's design to steal, kill and destroy—not God's. God's plans are to bless, not harm; to prosper, not to curse. We need to understand that it is He who asks that receives. We must ask, and we must ask for good things.

I'm a father, and though I'm painfully aware of my shortcomings in fatherhood, I still will give good things to my children. Jesus calls those of us who are fathers "evil" in comparison with the goodness of our Father in heaven. How much more will God, who is incapable of being evil, give good things to us, His children? God is not reluctant to give good things from His abundance to His children. He is eager for blessing and abundance for His children. Of all the good fathers we know, He supremely exceeds every one of us in all scope of what a generous father ought to be.

My own father never withheld from me when I was a child, and provided for us as a family in every possible way. This has helped me immensely with my concept of God in heaven. However, there are many people who had difficult experiences with their fathers, and this has left them with a picture of a withholding God unhappy with everything they do, never able to be satisfied, always finding fault.

The Bible presents a very different view of our Father in heaven. Our perception of God is what we will experience in life. In the parable of Luke 19, one of the servants who had received a pound from the Lord and did nothing with it, remarked that he had not followed the Lord's instructions with the pound because he knew the Lord to be "a hard man" (*NIV*). He had acted in fear. Not putting anything to risk, he simply hid the pound so he could give it back to the Lord when he was asked for it. God judged him according to his perception. The man saw God as hard, and so he experienced the severity of God. The pound was taken from him and given to another, who would multiply it. Yet God rewarded those who saw Him as good. Their faith inspired them to act in faith, trading with what they had been given.

When our perceptions change, so do our lives. We are transformed by the renewing of our minds (Romans 12:2). Remember: GOD IS GOOD!

9

IF
anyone
THIRSTS,
let him **COME TO ME**
and **DRINK.**

—John 7:37

drink

We each of us, parched mouths seek moisture.
We drink from wells poisoned,
Rivers muddied,
Fountains sour,
Waddies stagnant,
And Isaiah's voice
Cries across the centuries,
"Come, you thirsty, come drink."
Where? To whom?
At world's end the fountain found,
It's Him, Jesus, standing, crying,
On that last day
On that great day
On that feast Day
We come to Him,
We drink water sweeter than any anywhere,
Quenching a thirst we didn't know we had,
Used to it so long.
But now we drink, and drink, and drink,
and drink again,
Yet not satisfied, yet satisfied all,
Drink of Ages to You I come.

Effective prayer thirsts. IF anyone thirsts for God, they come to Him and "drink." How else can we come to Christ except through prayer? Apart from prayer, it's impossible to draw near to God. Old Testament priests drew near to God by passing through three sets of veils in the temple. They went from the outer court, through the Holy Place, and then into the Holy of Holies, where the High Priest met with God once a year on the Day of Atonement.

Jesus has made a whole new way for us where there are no veils or partitions. Quite simply we are able to enter all the way into the presence of God without hindrance, through His blood. As we draw near to God, He promises to draw near to us (see James 4:8). Our thirst is slaked through the presence of God. "Drinking" is praying, connecting with God himself. Jesus promised to fill us with the Spirit. We come to Christ thirsting, hungry for Him and all He has, without any apathy.

The half-hearted prayer receives nothing from God. Hunger and thirst for God needs to fill our prayers. Without a passion for God, our prayer life degenerates to just the fulfillment of religious obligations, lacking any real heart. We become those whose lips honor Him but whose hearts are far from Him (see Isaiah 29:13).

"Drinking" is taking in God. It is moving with whatever the Lord is doing. It is to take in what God is pouring out. We flow with whatever He is doing. If awe and wonder fills our soul, then we need to worship and praise. If laughter is in our soul, then we need to laugh. If weeping, then weep. If joy, then song. Praying, then, is also to "drink." Praying can be speaking in heavenly languages (tongues), "drinking in" the Spirit Jesus has promised.

10

ASK,

and it will be *given* to you;
seek,

and you will *find;*
knock, and IT WILL BE

opened to you.
For everyone who ASKS *receives,*
and he who seeks *finds,*
and to him who KNOCKS
it will be *opened.*
—*Luke 11:9–10*

seek

How simple can it be?
Ask…receive,
Knock…open,
Seek…find,
This life of seeking is always finding,
Asking, receiving,
Knocking, opening.
IF we don't, we won't receive, find or be opened to,
Yet IF we do…

How simple is this?! "Ask and you shall receive." It's hard to believe life could be that simple. The cynics scowl, "As if!" Yet here it is from the mouth of Jesus, the Son of God, by whom God has spoken. James 4:2 says that we don't have, because we don't ask. Many of us were reprimanded as children, "Don't ask!" However, here, our heavenly Father says, "Ask." It's time to ask of God those things you desire (see John 16:24).

Don't let those teachers who have no faith in the goodness of God convince you otherwise. They say things like, "God supplies your need, not your greed," as though anything outside the realm of your basic needs is greed. This is not Scripture. It is not the nature of God to withhold from His children. If He has not withheld Jesus, how will He withhold anything else good (see Romans 8:32)?

God is good! He purposes to bless people, not hurt them. We fail to believe this Scripture, "Ask and you shall receive," because we don't believe God is that good. We imagine He is unwilling to give us what we ask for, but this is exactly where our mind needs a revolution (the result of a revelation!). The revealed Word of God transforms our thinking, which gives us faith in the goodness of God. We get set free to ask Him for those things we desire.

11

If a **son** asks for bread from any **father** among you, will he give him a s t o n e? Or if he *asks* for a fish, will he give him a s e r p e n t instead of a fish? Or if he *asks* for an egg, will he offer him a scorpion? If **you then**, being evil, know how to give *good gifts* to your **children**, how much more will your **heavenly Father** give the *Holy Spirit* to those who *ask* Him!

—*Luke 11:11-13*

how much more

What is this language?
Where does it come from?
Not the ravings of occult chatterers,
Nor the chantings of rolled eye worshippers,
Nor the blood splattered tranced spiritists.
Nothing to fear, for,
God though whelming
Prevents short of overwhelming,
No losing control here.
Rather His gift within His gift, self-control.
He neither deceives nor disappoints.
This Father of ours exceeds.
He pours out to the hungry, the thirsty.
He pours out His Spirit.
He sends His great Presence to the seeking,
the asking.
Here He comes!
Fear not, the Father has sent Him.

W e don't need to fear the supernatural world of God. When we pray, we enter a supernatural world. In a world where anything supernatural is seen as having dark connotations, some are nervous about moving in that realm. But the spiritual and supernatural is where God lives. He is a Spirit (see John 4:24). He won't bring evil things into our lives in answer to our prayers. Some people think there is something sinister regarding the Holy Spirit and the power of God. Some teach that speaking in tongues is inspired by the devil, along with healing and deliverance. These are not new accusations. In Luke 11:15, Jesus

Himself was accused of using the power of the devil. His retort was that a Kingdom divided against itself is doomed (see Luke 11:17). [1]

Jesus is saying that if our children ask us for fish or bread, we don't give them serpents and stones. He is assuring us that if we ask God for the Holy Spirit, then that is what we will receive—the Holy Spirit, nothing less. When we ask for good things, that is what we will receive, good things, from God.

How much more… When the Spirit is poured into our lives it will be even more than what we expected. In fact, this is a normal response of heaven to our requests. He will give more than we have sought Him for. The supplies of God are inexhaustible. He never runs out. There's always more.

note

1. Nowhere in the entire New Testament is there any indication that these gifts have been withdrawn from believers.

12

Now to **HIM**
who is **ABLE** to do
EXCEEDINGLY
ABUNDANTLY
ABOVE ALL that we
ASK or **THINK,**
ACCORDING TO THE POWER
that **WORKS IN US**...
—*Ephesians 3:20*

exceedingly, abundantly

We dream, we pray,
We pray, we dream.
His answers.
Beyond our dreams,
Exceeding our faith,
Surprising our doubt,
Bending our knees
To Him, the merciful One,
Reading our hearts,
Answering our thoughts
The loud quiet of our mind reaches heaven
His delight to bless, not curse,
To exceed, not withhold,
To overflow, not just fill,
This is our God, no miser He,
Profuse and copious,
Plentiful forever, unlimited Provider,
We praise You!

Spirit plants vision and dreams within peoples' minds is because that vision becomes a creative force. It becomes a living prayer within a person's mind. It is a perception, a "seeing," of something invisible to the naked eye. In other words, it can be said that prayer creates.

*O*ur thinking and praying need to be aligned. Paul says here that God will answer us above what we ask OR think—not AND think.

Our thoughts are as loud as our prayers in heaven!

Our prayers are negated when our thinking contradicts them. This is the double-minded person of James 1:6-8. The first step in successful praying is aligning the prayers of our heart with the thoughts of our brain.

The word translated to "think" is the Greek word *noieo*, meaning "to perceive." We "see" things with our mind. The *NIV* translates this word as "imagine." The mind becomes a creative force when it begins imagining. The reason the Holy

The second great point in this Scripture is that our prayers will be exceeded by the Father. His nature is to over-supply His children. Abundance! He doesn't wish to withhold anything at all back from us. If He has given us His only Son, how can there possibly be anything of greater value that He would be holding back? If God has given us Jesus, there is nothing else He will not give to bless our lives.

He is the God of the overflowing abundance. The power that releases this abundance is the Holy Spirit. It is the same power that raised Jesus from the dead. This same power will cause the answers to our prayers to exceed all our expectations.

13

IF *two* of you
a g r e e on earth concerning
anything
that they ASK,
it w i l l b e d o n e for them
by *My Father in heaven.*
—*Matthew 18:19*

two

two

two

Just two to move a mountain,
Just two agreeing, believing.
Disharmony bars heaven,
Shuts down the white light of a future bright,
But those choosing unity over opinion,
Who sacrifice agenda to agreement,
Who love above grievance,
Those who heal the wounded breach,
Recovering love,
Discover the children choosing to agree.

God loves to answer those prayers of agreement. This is not some superstitious belief that if we say "we agree together," then we have fulfilled this requirement. This agreement must be authentic, it must be real. It is harmony of intention and purpose. The agreement is a "yes" coming from the soul. This "chemistry," this "hum," is what releases above normal power in business teams, rock bands, sporting teams, a marriage. Even two quarter horses harnessed together can pull up to three times the weight of that they can pull on their own.

Harmony is power.

The place of agreement is the place of power. This agreement (*sumphoneo* in Greek, which means "to be harmonious; in accord") taps into a power that releases heaven on earth.

The Lord's prayer begins with "Our Father," not "my father." Prayer is a corporate affair. Our power is in the harmony of relationships between those who pray. Unity begins with as small a number as just two.

The word "anything" offers us a spectacular horizon as big as our imagination.

14

And
WHATEVER
things you *ask* in *prayer,*
BELIEVING,
you **WILL**
receive.

—Matthew 21:22

whatever

A thing is a thing is a thing is a thing,
"Whatever" "things,"
He widens our dreams,
Could He mean it?
Dare I think it?
Can I believe it?
Ah, now there's the question.
There's the "rub."
Not the thing,
Not the "who,"
But "if" I can believe,
Conviction we'd die for,
Assurance we'd live through anything for,
Substance within, of reality unseen,
This is believing.

The essence of faith is receiving something before we actually have it. To know that a thing is yours before you actually possess it is an event that cheats the way our natural world works. This is the prayer of faith. "Believing" is the key to "effective" prayer. Without faith, prayer remains unanswered. Faith forms in us when we hear the Word of God. When we speak His Word, faith is injected into our prayers. We pray with faith. This is why it is imperative to speak the promises of God to ourselves. Scriptures like the one above impart faith into our soul when we speak them. Say it out loud right now! "I believe!" Faith will grow in your spirit.

Notice that God places zero restrictions on what we should pray for. He says, "whatsoever." It's His desire to fulfill our prayers. It is impossible to pray with faith to God for something evil. Prayer is, in itself, self-regulating. However, with Scriptures like this, God has opened our possibilities as wide as our faith, so we are unrestricted in our dreams for His Kingdom.

Therefore
I SAY TO **YOU**,
whatever things
you ask when you *pray*,
BELIEVE that you
receive them,
and you **WILL**
have them.

—*Mark 11:24*

receive

Do I have it?
Then it's mine.
I receive today what I do not have,
So I have tomorrow what I desire today,
It arrives before it arrives,
In my spirit it lives and moves,
Substance from the future,
A reality to walk by,
I own it today.
The title deed I have inside,
The guarantee
Of a future,
Based on a faith today.

thing is a thing! It can be anything! Whatever things we are praying for, we need to receive them WHEN we pray—not when we receive them. If we are waiting to receive what we have prayed for before we believe we have it, then we are not walking in faith. Faith doesn't walk by what it can see; it walks by what cannot be seen by the natural eye. It walks by the promise of God's Word. If God says I have the answer, then I have it—before I can see it. This is true regarding physical things like a circumstance, such as a house, a job, or a healing. It's also true regarding possibilities, like the kind where people say, "I can't see that happening." But instead of saying, "I can't see how it can happen," say, "I can see how it will happen"— even when you can't! Simply begin to believe instead of doubting. Start believing in prayer that you have the answers. Believe that you have it before you have it and you'll eventually have it. This is what is meant by becoming pregnant with a reality before it's born.

In Genesis 17:5, God told Abraham, "I have made you a father of many nations." Abraham had been made father of many nations before he even had one child, when his wife was barren and he was nearly one hundred years old. God didn't tell him he would be or that he is now, but that it was already done—past tense! "I have made you." It had already happened (see Romans 4:17). As far as God (who is the beginning and the ending of time) is concerned, Abraham's future was God's history, thus He could look back on what was yet to happen to his servant. This is what Abraham believed. Faith is what links us with our future. Our *faith* is the "substance of things hoped for" (see Hebrews 11:1).

When we receive today what we are hoping for tomorrow, we live with the assurance that we already have those things we dream of. This makes us walk and talk and plan and prepare a certain way. We live with a certainty of things others cannot see. We laugh at how impossible it looks, because we know within that we already have the reality.

16)

Until now
you have asked NOTHING in *My name.*
ASK, and YOU
will *receive,*
that your *joy* may be full.

—*John 16:24*

joy

joy

His name, our authority.
The name above all others,
Cries for employ.
Why does His name lay unused?
In that name nil can stand against,
Yet heaven under orders to open the unopened
At the mention of His name.
Why?
That joy reign over dismay,
Dreams fulfilled spill that happy rain through the earth,
Answered prayers relieve the sick, deliver the oppressed,
Lift the low, bring the ways of God to man,
And our joy lives.

*U*p until this time, the disciples have asked Jesus to get them across the lake, heal an epileptic child, explain parables, teach them to pray, and a host of other requests. But now He is about to depart. He is about to become the mediator and priest for them before God. He gives them the power to pray in His name—the ultimate Authority in heaven and earth. His name carries total authority in the universe, and He is happy to give that to us, His disciples, to use in making requests and issuing commands.

Many of the artists of the Renaissance and other periods used apprentices to paint parts or sometimes even entire works, which they then put their name to. The young painters were to paint "in the name" of the master. His style, his coloring, his techniques, were all to be imitated by the apprentice. As we "paint" the world with the Kingdom that Jesus calls us to bring, we are functioning in His name. His Spirit comes upon us and we say and do those things He would do in any circumstance. As we give ourselves to live in His name and to pray in His name, His power enables us to accomplish divine purposes in the earth.

This passage also reveals that He wants us to ask. He is saying that if you have been slack in asking, now is the time to begin requesting things so that your joy is not incomplete. Our joy cannot be full as long as our families remain unsaved, as long as people we love endure illness, as long as those we care for are impoverished. As long as we own compassion, her joy begs to be fulfilled through her desires being accomplished.

Yet **YOU** DO NOT HAVE
because
YOU DO NOT **ASK**.
—*James 4:2*

ask

We hope, we wish and still nothing,
We ache, we pine, still nothing,
We moan, we groan, still nothing,
We enlist, we deploy, still nothing,
We want, we want, we want, still nothing,
Why does He not stop this, start that?
An answer too simple to believe;
Did we Ask?
Ask, Ask, and Ask again.

*H*ow many times have
you lost your keys, spent thirty
minutes looking for them, then
thought about asking God to show
you where they are?

How many times have we liked
something but not asked for it
because we were unsure whether
we should have it?

How many times have we not asked
for help because we thought we
could do it on our own?

How many times have we done
something without asking God
about it and afterward wish we had...

asked about buying those shares,

about buying that house,

about that new car,

about going into partnership with
that person,

about even marrying that person.

The reason we don't have wisdom,
guidance, empowerment, is simply
because we have not asked for it.

Jesus says, "Ask, and receive."

You ask
and DO NOT RECEIVE,
because you ask amiss,
that you may
spend it on your pleasures.
—*James 4:3*

ask right

We know it's wrong, but we ask anyway,
We have no faith, but we ask anyway,
We're embarrassed to ask, but we do anyway.
We don't receive, because we can't.
Our spirit opens to the will of God.
Independent from Him, faith is not faith at all,
His will, our will, aligned bring pleasures from there, not here.

One reason for unanswered prayer is that the request is self-centered. We want the thing for our own pleasure, not God's. The secret of the Kingdom of God is that He is the first priority, and everything in our lives is shaped by Him being at the center, rather than us. In this environment He has no problem "adding" to us what He has promised.

Remember, God is love (see John 4:8). If He chooses to not answer our prayer, it's because the request is outside of His love for us.

This highlights that it is not the prayer God answers, it's the person. Two people can pray for the same thing. One receives it, the other does not.

At the center of one heart is God, at the other is self. It is the Joshua generation that possesses the promised land. The old generation had to die before they could take what God had for them. Our old nature with selfishness at its core must die. Then our intentions spring from a purified heart. One person is praying for a larger house so they can be hospitable to people, to have people to stay there who need help. Another prays for a large house simply because the idea of it appeals to their ego. Their intention is to impress. They want to consume it all on themselves.

It's God's honor when His children are blessed. He will pour abundance out upon those who live for His glory, and not theirs.

19)

And **W H A T E V E R**
we *ask*
WE **R E C E I V E**
from Him,
because we **KEEP** His COMMANDMENTS
and do those things that are
P L E A S I N G in His sight.
—*1 John 3:22*

obedience

Living right, confident like sun rising,
Pleasing Him, we're a garden of roses,
We're cedars of Lebanon,
His pleasure smiles in our soul,
We conceive answers,
We commune,
Deep calling out,
What we do uprights our soul,
Standing bold, prayers become answers.

*A*nswered prayer is the manifestation of a hidden life of obedience. It is not the nature of the prayer that impresses God; it's the life of the person praying. God had respect toward Abel first, then toward his offering. The offering is secondary to God. If the life is right, so will the offering be right. Abel gained God's attention through his obedience in bringing the offering prescribed by God and by doing what was pleasing to God.

Faith pleases God.

The word "whatever" continually surfaces when the Bible speaks of prayer. If our lives are right, it hardly matters what we pray for, God's pleasure is to give His kingdom to those who please Him.

But *FROM THERE*
you **will**
seek the **LORD** your **GOD**,
and YOU WILL FIND HIM
if
you **SEEK HIM** with
ALL YOUR HEART
and with
ALL YOUR SOUL.
—*Deuteronomy 4:29*

seek him

IF you seek Him with all your heart…
We find our loves,
We seek our loves,
He's the passion, the prize,
Discovered by the heart thirsty,
Revealed to the heart seeking,
None other, none else,
None higher, none at all,
He alone claiming our utmost, our all;
And we find, not His hand, but Himself.
When we seek from wherever, whenever,
He cares not,
Just that we seek Him.

The context of this passage is a prophecy referring to the future dispersion of the Jewish people throughout all the earth. God assures them that even though they are scattered far away from their promised land because of their sins against Him, if they seek Him from those places with all their heart and soul, they will find Him.

We do not have to be in some special place to find God. He is found anywhere on this earth by anyone fully engaging their heart and soul.

We seek God because we want to find Him. When we drift from God, we can and need to rediscover Him. How? Get alone, put time aside, and seek Him with all you have.

Crises hit our lives to awaken us. Pain gets our attention. We stir our heart to seek God. He seeks our attention more than our comfort. If He has to sacrifice our comfort to gain our attention, then so be it.

It's impossible for the casual heart to find God. If God is to be revered, then the only person to whom He will reveal Himself is the wholehearted. If we don't really care whether we find Him or not, then we won't. But if we are desperate for God, we will find Him. He will make Himself known to the passionate heart.

21

Uzziah was sixteen years old when he became **king**, and he reigned fifty-two years in Jerusalem. His mother's name was Jecholiah of Jerusalem.

And he did what was **right** in the sight of the LORD, ACCORDING TO ALL THAT **HIS FATHER** AMAZIAH HAD DONE.

He **sought** God in the days of Zechariah, who had UNDERSTANDING in the *visions* **of God**; and AS LONG AS HE **SOUGHT** THE LORD, God made him *PROSPER*

—*2 Chronicles 26:3-5*

prosper

Sixteen and a king,
Fathered and cared for,
Amaziah and Zechariah
King makers of the young.
Towering in history Uzziah reigns,
Under the reign of Yahweh.
Fifty two long successful years,
Why?
He sought Yahweh.
He found prosperity.
Zechariah heard.
He spoke what he heard.
Uzziah prayed what the prophet declared.
His mother's embrace, his father's words, Zechariah's prayers,
Echoed in his throne,
Shepherding Israel to blessing.

Second Chronicles 26:9-15 tells of how Uzziah masterminded the construction of fortress towers in Jerusalem at various points on the walls. He also undertook massive agricultural projects in the desert as well as the foothills and plains. He reorganized an army of 307,500 men into well-trained and well-equipped divisions under 2,600 leaders. He pioneered the use of advanced weapons such as catapults to hurl arrows and large stones a great distance. All this enhanced his reputation and increased his strength.

His secret to his enormous success is that he sought God. Zechariah the prophet inspired King Uzziah with deep and clear insights. Zechariah saw visions of God. He interpreted these to the king. The prophet's influence aroused the king to seek the Lord. As long as he did so, the great king prospered.

Scripture is plain: As long as King Uzziah sought God, he prospered. The inference is clear. When we cease to seek God, we also cease to prosper (see 2 Chronicles 26:16-18).

*U*zziah sits as a grand king in the history of Judah. His accomplishments equal the greatest of leaders.

Alongside the first mention of Uzziah acceding the throne is the record that he rebuilt a town called Eloth, which was on the shore of the Red Sea in the land of Edom (see 2 Chronicles 26:2). Eloth was a supremely strategic port, from which Judah was able to establish herself in a formidable position in the years to come. Uzziah also destroyed the Philistine towns of Gath, Jabneh, and Ashdod. He rebuilt other cities in the region to consolidate his victories. He succeeded in military campaigns against the Arabs of Gur Baal and the Meunites (see 1 Chronicles 4:41; 2 Chronicles 26:6-8). The Ammonites recognized his sovereignty over them, and his fame spread to Egypt's borders.

22

Let the *hearts* of those *rejoice* who s e e k the LORD!
S e e k the LORD and HIS STRENGTH;
SEEK His *face evermore*
—*1 Chronicles 16:10-11*

rejoice
The nations cry for joy.
Just one drop of elusive joyfulness.
To celebrate without a reason,
To be happy even without.
The world crawls through the mire.
Imagining pleasure brings joy.
Ahh, empty bottle,
Dry bread and sour milk.
Fix your heart, weary soul,
Bolt your eyes to heaven,
Imprison your soul in prayer,
From there joy springs,
Laughter even.
Reason enough to seek Him forevermore.

*T*hree times the word "seek"
appears in 1 Chronicles 16:10-11.

The heart of the problem is always the
problem of the heart. Even when we
face severe challenges to our attitudes,
if we are God-seekers, then we are
rewarded with joy. The strength of our
heart is the joy of the Lord. Drawing
close to God is drawing close to joy.

Joy comes from seeking the Lord.
People seeking joy should spend time
seeking the Lord. This is saying that
even just the seeking (not necessarily
the finding) of God brings a joy
unavailable with any other pursuit in life.

When we are weak, we are
strengthened if we seek the Lord.
His strength is available if we will
collect it. Prayer says we are weak
without God, but with Him we
are strengthened. IF we seek Him,
we become strong with a strength
exceeding anything we can conjure.

The psalmist urges us to seek His face
forever. Our eternal purpose should
be to seek the face of almighty God.
If our face is towards Him perpetually
and continually, if we have set our
face towards God's face and will not
turn to the right or to the left, but let
our eyes look straight ahead, then we
will experience the purest of joys and
come to reflect His face to the world
we live in.

23

Now set your *heart* and your *soul* to s e e k the LORD your God. Therefore A R I S E and **BUILD** the sanctuary of the LORD God, to bring the *ark of the covenant of the LORD* and the *holy articles of God* into the **HOUSE** that is to be **BUILT** for the name of the LORD.

—*1 Chronicles 22:19*

pray and build

We build a place to sleep,
A place to eat,
A place to rest,
A place to gather, to sit,
To study, to wash,
To cook, to play.
Yet, a place to pray?
To seek and wait.
Build this place for Him. For you.
Build a place for His presence.
A place for the ark.
This presence is your title to blessing.
Your title to joy.

We must make the commitment to seek the Lord. Without commitment we easily drift from prayer. Throughout our life, our face needs to point toward heaven, undistracted by the good or the bad.

People who seek God build places for God. They want His presence established permanently in the earth. This presence is a presence of covenant. We build a place for His covenant to be established. This place—the House of God—is that place where the "holy articles" (gifted people) find their destiny, their place, their purpose.

24

And **he** [Rehoboam] **did evil**, because **he did not prepare** his heart to seek the LORD.

—*2 Chronicles 12:14*

prepare to pray

One prepares for Him,
Another does not.
One does right,
The other does not.
Rehoboam, so many mistakes,
Had you sought Him,
Your folly would die.
Yet your heart had no desire, no ache,
For God,
And so evil wiled it's way,
Entwining your defenseless heart.
Estranging you from Him,
Alienating you from your destiny, your people, your God.

*I*n contrast to Uzziah, Rehoboam did not seek the Lord and, consequently, he did evil. The influence of his Ammonite mother swayed his decisions, so he found himself behaving badly.

IF we pray, we are empowered to do right instead of wrong. The influence of the wrong crowd—even if they are family—evaporates. Prayer causes us to be influenced by heaven. Prayer transforms us so we can change our world.

25

He **commanded** Judah to **s e e k** the LORD
God of their fathers, and to **observe** the **law** and the
commandment.
—*2 Chronicles 14:4*

commanded to pray

What's a leader for?
To pray, to hear, to obey.
Knowing the power, the secret, Asa changes everything.
His people changed their world.
They sought the Lord.
Why?
Their leader required it.
He commanded it!
Their power to perform His law discovered in prayer.

Sometimes we are inspired from within that we need to seek the Lord, but mostly throughout Bible history, God's people seek God only because they have been told to by their leaders.

*A*sa is among the greatest Kings of Jewish history. He breaks with his lineage of bad leaders and begins a new legacy of noble leadership for Judah. He commands the entire nation to seek the Lord.

This is the power of leaders who seek the Lord. They influence all those following to do the same. We don't always need to just feel "moved" to prayer. It's enough at times to follow the example of leaders who themselves seek the Lord and obey the call to pray.

26

Then they *entered* into a **covenant** to **s e e k** the LORD God of their fathers with all their *heart* and with all their *soul* ; and whoever would **not s e e k** the LORD God of Israel was to be P U T   T O   D E A T H, whether *small* or **great**, whether **man** or *woman*.

—*2 Chronicles 15:12-13*

covenant of prayer

Serious days when you die failing to pray,
Such was their passion,
Such was their resolve.
It's a covenant we make with each other.
We'll pray, or else we die!
Thousands depend on us praying.
If we wait to feel it, we won't;
If we wait for convenience, zero!
But if we will commit to every day,
Traveling through the veil,
For our people, ourselves,
Then answers from heaven fall
And we are all saved.

Asa's reign is marked by the amount of times he and the people committed themselves to seek the Lord. His good influence is long lasting upon the successive leaders of Judah. Anyone who seeks the Lord will influence many people beyond their own immediate sphere, both presently and in the future.

*K*ing Asa brought massive reform throughout Judah. Until in the fifteenth year of his reign he led his people into a commitment to seek God—with dire consequences for any who refused (see 2 Chronicles 15:10-15).

The Kingdom of God doesn't offer any neutral ground. We're either in or out. Here, everyone felt a corporate responsibility to carry out the purposes of their King, to seek the Lord. They wanted complete unity, so death was threatened to any who refused to seek the Lord.

This oath didn't produce fear, but rather immense joy and celebration throughout the nation. They discovered God when they sought Him with all their heart. Joy comes to the surrendered heart. The half-hearted can never have the buoyancy that comes from the heart fully given to the Lord.

Asa's seriousness about the matter was such that he called the entire nation into a commitment to seek the Lord (and anyone who didn't want to be put to death). The covenant applied to every person, young, old, small or great, rich or poor. The result was great joy. Because anyone who makes a biding commitment to the highest of purposes (seeking God) is going to find themselves experiencing great joyfulness.

27

And in the thirty-ninth year of his reign, Asa became diseased in his feet, and his malady was SEVERE; yet in his disease he did not s e e k the LORD, but the physicians. So Asa rested with his fathers; he D I E D in the forty-first year of his reign.

—*2 Chronicles 16:12-13*

God first

Asa, you amaze me.
One moment, "Pray or die, people,"
Next, physicians first, maybe God later.
Even the great falter and forget.
When we ignore Him and prefer paltry man.
In our unease, or disease, we should seek the Lord.
Always some malady discomforts us,
And in this we must seek the Lord.
We anger Him, who can do it all.

*T*his tragic passage reveals one of the giants of leadership failing to do the very thing that made him successful. From the beginning of his reign he sought the Lord and called upon his nation to do the same. Yet, when he faced this terrible personal problem in the evening of his life he did not seek God, but only his doctors. There is no problem with us seeking help from doctors, but God needs to be the first we seek for a miracle. Asa died because he didn't seek the Lord to heal him, and would have lived if he had.

Even good men cut short their influence when they fail to seek the Lord. Who knows how many years of positive influence Asa lost by not simply seeking the Lord when he became sick.

Uzziah sought God in the days of Zechariah the prophet. Whenever a leader is surrounded with "God influences" they will be drawn towards God. Every leader needs people who walk close to God and will also walk close to them.

The most amazing point in Asa's life is that even though his reign was marked by the words "sought the Lord," his greatest mistake was that privately he did not seek the Lord first when he contracted a disease in his feet.

Second Chronicles 16 tells the story of another mistake Asa made, which was that he formed an alliance with Ben Hadad I of Damascus, purchasing their favor with temple treasures. This was identified as a lack of faith by a local prophet named Hanani (whom Asa then imprisoned for telling him this).

The message of seeking God is good, but it's not all we need to be engaged in. Faith is essential to our prayer life. It is the prayer of faith that affects miracles. Faith expressed in prayer is what releases God's power over our circumstances.

Asa should have believed God and not sought the assistance of another king. He should have sought God first, rather than the physicians in the days of his illness, and his reign would not have been cut short.

28

Then the **children** of Israel who had
returned from the captivity ate *together* with
all who had **S E P A R A T E D** themselves from the
filth of the nations of the land in order to **S E E K**
the **LORD God of Israel.**
—*Ezra 6:21*

separated to pray

Dragging feet,
Sticky ground,
Defiled and unclean our lives drone.
Brass altars and lavers are passage to the inner chamber.
Separated and clean we walk into glory.
Only the cleansed can come.
Jesus' blood available for all,
Yet not all will take it.
Those who will, will seek, and find. Him.

*O*nce we have been set free from our "captivity," we should separate ourselves to God so we become clean. Seeking God is both a reason and a result. To seek God cleanses us from the unclean. Encounters with God cleanse and purify us.

When Isaiah the prophet entered the Presence of the Lord, his lips, touched with fire from heaven, emerged purified. When Joshua the High Priest was before the Lord in Zechariah, his "filthy garments" were replaced with the clean. Seeking God cleanses our lives. Cleansed, we are ushered into His presence. The stains of the world are lifted from our soul. Heaven's air breathes in our frame.

29

The young **lions** LACK AND SUFFER HUNGER;
But those who seek the **LORD** shall
NOT LACK ANY *good thing.*
—*Psalm 34:10*

no lack

Even the prowling young king,
Brilliant in capture,
Lightning in strike,
Feared and undefeated,
Even he gapes with lack in famine days.
But seekers of God,
Ah, now there's the thing;
These will lack nothing.
The best will be theirs in the worst of times.

*P*rovision flows to those seeking God. Seeking God brings inspiration to our minds. We receive ideas that tap resources. God pours provisions our way just because we seek Him! Merely seeking Him dispenses provision into our world.

Even those who should not suffer hunger—those who are the "king" of their "jungle," the strong, the youthful lions—will encounter times that are so difficult that even they will suffer lack. However, no matter what the circumstances, those who seek God will never lack for anything. And not just our needs—God will not allow us to lack any good thing, simply because we seek Him. The desires and dreams of our heart are made reality. Any good thing we are hoping for will come to us as we seek the Lord.

30

EVIL MEN do not understand justice,
But those who seek the LORD understand all.
—*Proverbs 28:5*

understanding

understanding

Insight escapes the mind dark with dark plans,
Deep selfishness fails fairness,
But the mind intent on Christ,
Nods to lady justice,
Even her scales tip against us.
Being right even if wrong,
Higher than cheating the lady blind.

"Understanding" is key to leading and relating to people and to navigating our way through life. As we seek God and think on a situation needing answers, we will see what we need to do, and will understand how to accomplish good results. Seeking God opens our mind to all the possibilities around us. It transforms our thinking into a positive mindset so we discover ways to touch other people's lives and be a blessing in this world.

People who seek God, receive insight into events that appear unjust. So, instead of becoming cynical and bitter, their hearts fail to be hardened. People who do not seek God have no defense in their soul; so when justice is meted out in life, they see it as unfair. They refuse to accept that there is any right in God's actions.

31

Woe to those who go down to Egypt for help,
And rely on horses,
Who trust in chariots because they are many,
And in horsemen because they are very strong,
But who do not look to the HOLY ONE of Israel,
Nor seek the LORD!

—*Isaiah 31:1*

seek the Lord

Under threat, our glance to the side,
Threatens our gaze to above.
Lift your chin, set your eyes on high.
The many, the strong, no guarantee at all.
Apart from Him we can do nothing.
Our woes are our own.
We escaped prayer, embracing logic.
Thus we escaped victory, embracing woe.
I release my grip on the many, the strong,
To grasp my King, my God.

All of us need help at some time or another. We need help for a thousand and one situations. We offend God when we seek this world's help instead of His. "Woe" covers the wide range of distress, misfortune, unhappiness, loss, failure, disaster, remorse, difficulty, disfavor, and one bad thing after another befalling our lives. All these things covered in the word "woe" will be ours if we ignore God in our distress and only seek help from people.

When we imagine that we can get "stuff" from people and that God cannot give, we are wrong. There is no one and nothing in this world that even begins to equal the power, the abundance, the strength, and the resources that are available in God.

Our needs are meant in order to move us to God. Our need should move us to look to Him for rescue, shelter, and help.

32

Seek the LORD while He *may be found,*
Call upon Him while *He is near.*

—*Isaiah 55:6*

Feel that calling,
That drawing?
It's quiet, even silent;
Don't ignore it.
Stop everything!
Come aside.
Seek Him, when He calls.
In the valley, on the mountain,
Wherever,
No matter the inconvenience,
The embarrassment to ego,
The difficulty to explain,
No matter what,
Drop it now.
Seek Him. He's near!

There are times we know we need to return to the Lord—if not in our whole lives, then at least in a particular area. We are arrested with the conviction that we need to return to God. We begin seeking God. In this environment, both the wicked and the unrighteous find mercy in abundance. God draws near to us when we seek Him. Here we find repentance, faith, and healing.

*T*here are definitely times when God is nearer than others. Why remain a mystery. There are times when we know God is exceptionally near and able to be found. In these moments we need to abandon all distractions and lesser pursuits, and make the pursuit of God our primary work. Of all the opportunities we have, this is the greatest. When God draws us to Himself, we should chase after Him with all our heart.

33

Sow for yourselves **righteousness**;
Reap in mercy;
B r e a k up your fallow ground,
For it is time to **seek** the **LORD**,
Till **He** comes and *rains* **righteousness** on you.
—*Hosea 10:12*

broken

Seeking Him, unsoftened, is fruitless.
Our proud, hard hearts must break.
Our time to seek Him has come,
Thus also the time to moisten the crusty surface,
To bow the stiffened neck,
Crumble the stony soul.
And seek Him with loamy hearts we will,
All the way,
Until He comes,
Bringing rains with Him.

Seeking God is a lifetime commitment. He does not call us to simply seek Him for ten minutes, thirty minutes, or an hour a day. He calls us to seek Him "until"…until we receive what we are seeking Him for.

Our rightness in life does not come from our actions. It comes from the Lord. As we seek Him, eventually He will come. When He comes, He makes our lives right. When God draws near, righteousness rains upon us.

Sincere believers often wrestle with accusations from the devil. However, when we seek God, instead of judgment raining down on us, righteousness pours from heaven.

Seeking God breaks up unused areas of our heart. It is impossible to seek God for any length of time without our heart softening. The very act of seeking God softens our heart. At some point that softness draws God like rain upon us. Then the seeds within sprout, and we reap the harvest.

34

Seek the **LORD** and *live.*

—Amos 5:6

live

"Life," where to find it?
In pleasure, in success?
In love, in war?
When am I truly alive?
When do my bones sing?
When am I breathless?
When does my soul rise to kiss heaven?
When do the stars shout
And the sun roar?
When does my red blood surge?
When does energy engage endless?
When does lemon brighten to yellow?
When?
When I seek Him!
That's where "life" is found.
Here this whole earth,
Searching for that life,
Everywhere but.

Only God has "life." It is only from God that we can get life. There is no other source of life in the entire universe. We access this life by seeking Him. The command is simple, straightforward, and completely unconfusing. It is, "Seek God and live!"

This endows us with a defense against legitimate judgment. Those who are seeking God with all their heart will avert judgments on their lives—judgments that no one could normally prevent.

35

The inhabitants of one city shall go to another, saying,
"Let us **continue** to *go and pray* before the **LORD**,
And s e e k the **LORD** of hosts.
I myself will go also."
Yes, many peoples and **STRONG NATIONS**
Shall come to s e e k the **LORD** of hosts in Jerusalem,
And to *pray* before the **LORD**.
—*Zechariah 8:21-22*

let's pray

"Come," they cry.
"For what?" we say.
"To pray."
Even I will go.
The strong will go.
The many will go.
A revival spreads
Coast to coast.
Revival is prayer.
It's there we touch the cities, the nations, the many.

Not just a few, but we live in a day when "many" will come to seek the Lord. The prayer meeting has traditionally been the poor cousin of church meetings; however, the day is coming when it will be the foremost of meetings. The prayer meeting has also been the domain of the unknown, the poorer members of the church, the older ones, sometimes the "unusual" ones.

The strong seem to have stayed away, but the day is coming when seeking the Lord will become the domain of the strong; and not just a few here and there, but entire nations that are considered to be strong will come and seek the Lord.

*I*nfluence increases for those who seek God. They bring others on the same journey. In fact, entire cities begin to influence one another to go to the House of God to pray and to seek the Lord. Instead of expecting that everyone else will go and pray, and looking on from the side, even those who would not normally go will say, "I myself will also go."

36

"After this I *will return*
And will **rebuild** the tabernacle of David, which has fallen down;
I will **rebuild** its ruins,
And I will SET IT UP;
So that the *rest of mankind* may s e e k the LORD,
Even all the Gentiles who are *called by My name*,"
Says the LORD who does all these things.
—*Acts 15:16-17*

rest of mankind

Why you, David?
Why your tent?
From heaven Yahweh hears your worship,
Reads hearts of love,
Is drawn near.
No one more magnetic than He,
The drawing power of His presence
Overwhelms reason,
And all the world seeks the Lord.

The reason God rebuilds David's tent (not Moses' or Solomon's) is to restore praise and worship. However, we should not stop at the first gate of the tent with only thanksgiving. We take the entire journey into the Holy of Holies, into the presence of God. We travel through thanksgiving for what He has done for us, to praise Him for what He does, to worship for who He is—regardless of whether He does anything at all. This level of worship brings that atmosphere where people seek the Lord. The culture of prayer in the House of God becomes the practice of everyone else entering the Kingdom. God is looking for the day when all mankind look for Him.

37

If you s e e k Him, He will be *found* by you; but if you FORSAKE Him, He will *cast you off* forever.
—*1 Chronicles 28:9*

if you seek him

Unteasing promises to those of "if."
To forsake is not to seek.
Seeking discovers.
Discovers Him.
How can we know Him the unknown,
Without seeking?
Come, we cry,
Relationship, nil religion,
Yet we languish in a land of not knowing,
Castaways with no traction.
Engage your heart, engage Him.
No reasons ever strong enough to leave off seeking.
Revive prayer quickly. Today. Now!

*T*hose who have decided to seek the Lord will find Him. He manifests Himself to us, empowering us to build for Him.

Forsaking God is placed in contrast to seeking Him. When we cease to seek God, He treats that as forsaking Him. If we do forsake Him because some other thing (a "god") has captured our heart, then God will cast us off forever. The fear of God should inspire us to seek Him as much as the inspiration of finding Him and all that He brings with Him.

Seekers of God become builders for God. They build up the church, rather than tear her down. They lift people up, rather than put them down. They exalt, rather than debase. They progress, rather than retreat.

The strength we need to build the church fills us when we wait on Him. The church is born and built by the Spirit. The church is a supernatural organism. We cannot build something spiritual by natural means. Whatever is born of the flesh is flesh, and whatever is born of the Spirit is spirit (John 3:6). We need supernatural strength to build the House of God. People enter the church through being born again. This can only happen through the power of the Holy Spirit. People are called, gifted, and sent by the power of the Spirit. The war the church grows in is too furious and too vicious for us to be able to live above it without greater strength than our own.

God is found by God seekers. He allows Himself to be revealed to those who set out to seek Him.

If we do not seek Him (in other words, if we forsake Him), then He also will do to us what we have done to Him—reject, cast away, and refuse to seek us.

God is not immediately discoverable. It is His glory to be hidden, and it is the glory of man to seek Him out (see Proverbs 25:2). People would love to find God in their world, yet the price is seeking Him with all we have.

38

Hear me, Asa, and all Judah and Benjamin. The LORD is with you while *you are with Him.* If you S E E K Him, He will be *found* by you; but if you F O R S A K E Him, He will F O R S A K E you.

—*2 Chronicles 15:2*

with him

He moves with us.
We move, He moves.
We draw close, so does He.
We leave Him, He leaves us.
We cleave to him, He to us.
We abide in Him, He in us!
Let all the world seek the Lord!

Himself to us can only be discovered when we seek Him. When we seek God, we are embracing Him. Seeking God connects us with the Father. While we seek Him, He is "with" us throughout our life.

*B*eing close to God depends not on Him but on us. When we stop seeking the Lord, we are forsaking Him. Any of us can be as close to God as we want. If you draw near to Him, He will draw near to you. IF we seek Him, we will find Him. Whichever way He wants to manifest

39

The hand of our God is upon all those for good who seek Him.
—*Ezra 8:22-23*

hand of God

We crave the good.
Good days,
Good life,
Good things.
The fountain of good,
Unstopped every morning.
Covering our days,
Blessing our nights,
With a hand,
A hand resting on us, for good.

zra was about to make the journey of 900 miles back to Jerusalem to rebuild both the city and the temple, carrying great amounts of treasure, gold, and silver. This included 25 tons of silver, plus silver objects weighing 3.75 tons, gold weighing 3.75 tons, 20 bowls of gold that weighed about 19 pounds, and two valuable bronze objects. All this was worth hundreds of millions of dollars in today's currency. And back then, highways didn't lack bandits and robbers willing to steal from travelers on the route.

Ezra had publicly claimed to the king and the people of Persia that God would protect and care for them, so he was embarrassed to ask for a band of soldiers to accompany them. So Ezra called on all the people to fast and pray, and God answered by protecting every step they took returning to Jerusalem.

The hand of God can deliver either blessing or judgment. Seeking God invokes His hand upon our lives, blessing us with good. Those who seek Him, discover how good God can be. Ezra records that they began to fast and pray for that good to be present in their extremely difficult circumstances. The results were immediate. They started and finished their journey in complete safety. God answered their prayer.

When we are nervous about our safety and the protection of our family and possessions, we can seek the Lord to provide His covering in dangerous circumstances, and He will answer us.

40

This is Jacob, the generation of those who seek Him, Who seek Your face.

—*Psalm 24:6*

the generation

Jacob, my friend,
Desperate man,
More desperate than any.
Desperate to die?
You fight God?
Yet you live?
Blessed, you leave the matted patch,
Limping, glowing, blessed.
Changed forever,
No longer swindling.
Princely you walk,
Noble your face,
Lame, your leg.
Desperate people, this generation.
Desperate for God.

At the end of his bout with God, Jacob's name was changed to "Israel," which means "he prevails as a prince with God." He also walked away from the encounter with a limp that remained for the rest of his life. He paid a price for the blessing on his life, and he accepted it without complaint.

Our wrestle is not to be only motivated by prayer because we need something, or because we're in trouble, or because we're desperate for our dreams to happen. Our greatest reason for seeking God is so we can find Him for Him—not just because of what He can do for us. Not only are we seeking Him, but we are eager to see His face. We seek His smile on our lives with blessings from heaven and grace that covers our shortcomings.

*S*eeking God is not a passive exercise. Jesus tells us the Kingdom of heaven is "taken" by force by aggressive (or "violent") people (see Matthew 11:12). Even at the outset, it's a fight to get motivated to pray. It takes a lot more than just good intentions to actually connect with God, and then to persist in seeking Him until we break through. This is exactly what Jacob did when God met him that night at Peniel. When we're prepared to wrestle for blessing, we will be blessed. Seeking God takes more than just a few short prayers. When we ignore our own comfort to increase the blessing of God upon us, we are in the company of Jacob. When blessing holds a higher value to us than anything else, we will seek Him at any price.

41

Blessed are those who
keep His testimonies,
Who seek Him with the whole
heart!
—*Psalm 119:2*

wholehearted

seeking

No heart finds Him,
But the whole heart.
Divided hearts only find Him elusive.
Like a woman married,
He shares our love with no other.
And so He blesses the given heart,
Withholding naught, but loving.

Prayer isn't a technical exercise we engage in once a day or once a week. When prayer degenerates to empty-hearted religion, we fool ourselves that we are fulfilling our calling. Seeking God is born from passion. We divert our focus and desires from other lesser attachments when we seek Him with all our heart. When our excitement for something else exceeds our passion for God, we must reawaken our hearts to Him as the first excitement of our life.

*B*lessing is promised to every person who sets their heart to seek the Lord.

To keep God's Word is to seek Him. To seek Him is to keep His Word. Obedience to God is not the easiest venture to embark on. Even the greatest heroes of Bible throughout church history had to be challenged with the call to obedience. Jesus Himself faced this challenge when the cross loomed before Him. He prayed for a way to avoid it, but while He sought God in Gethsemane, He also discovered strength to obey the call to the cross (see Matthew 26:39). Our strength to obey comes in prayer.

42

Where has your *beloved* gone,
O fairest among women?
Where has your *beloved* turned aside,
That we may s e e k him with you?
—*Song 6:1*

seek him with you

We value little what we have not lost.
Clearer we see Him,
Bolder we declare Him,
Our boast is high, though gone from us.
The daughters hear our script,
The song painting his frame.
Stirred, they refuse denial,
"We too will seek Him with you."

Is our song compelling?
Do our words arouse?
Is He lifted within us?
Then He draws, He draws, He draws.

he Song of Solomon is not an easy book to understand. The best take I can get on this romantic story is that Solomon has seen the plight of the girls he has selected from around the nation to be in his "harem." He has approximately one thousand wives and concubines. Even though he continues to amass this great bevy of beautiful women and they gain a place in his kingdom, he sometimes empathizes with their losses. He seems to be aware of one that had a boyfriend, a shepherd boy whom she loved with all her heart. Yet, when Solomon's scouts invited her to the palace promising wealth, jewels, comfort and the prestige of being one of the king's women, she left the countryside and her boyfriend. However, she spends her days pining for her lost lover and can't help but speak of him to the other girls. She dreams of him on her bed at night. It's a picture of us losing Jesus when we pursue the world.

When the Shulamite maiden describes her lover (Jesus) the other young beautiful women in Solomon's harem are inspired. They ask her to take them to him. At this point she herself doesn't know where he is. She has lost him, it seems. She has aroused the desire in herself as she talks about him and then her companions want to seek him as well, simply because she has described Him so wonderfully.

The church is described as the fairest among all women. This is because she is in relationship with Christ. The church looks awesome and beautiful when she is deeply connected with Christ. Sadly, too often she has appeared anything but, simply because she is disconnected. The connection happens when we seek God. Those who commune with God will also draw others into communion with Him.

43

And the **PRIDE** of Israel testifies to his face,

But they do not return to the LORD their God,

Nor *seek* Him for all this.

—*Hosea 7:10*

humble yourselves

Hell gapes for the proud.
Trouble besets them all round.
"Yet we will not pray,
yet we will not seek Him."
The lifted nose,
The puffed breast,
And concrete mind,
Wry, sour smile,
Imagining your defenses secure,
Smashed in a moment,
Yet you do not turn.
"No, we will not pray."
Fools, we die in our pride,
Unwilling humility,
Wallflower in our dance,
Withered from our soul,
Until we bow low and seek Him.

Let's bow down to God. Let's lift
hands to God. Let's break open our
hearts and seek the Lord, confessing
our shortcomings and seeking grace,
mercy, and forgiveness from Him.
God will not despise the humble
heart. He draws near to the humble,
but resists the proud.

ride is a wall against prayer
and seeking God. Our independence
has its roots in an arrogance that
refuses to bow the knee, fall on our
face, and declare that our greatest
need is for God Himself to touch our
lives and live within us.

"Help us, Lord, to come with humble
hearts and seek Your grace and power
for our lives."

Even though the Israelites were
chastised with pain and trouble, their
pride still would not let them seek
the Lord.

Seeking God brings humility to
our hearts. We need this more than
anything. If we are just half smart, we
will overcome our pride and begin to
pray, no matter how much it injures
our ego. This is the best medicine our
heart can take.

44

But *without* **faith** it is *impossible* to **please Him**, for he who *comes to God* must *believe that He is*, and that **He** is a *rewarder* of those who **diligently seek** Him.

—*Hebrews 11:6*

faith faith *faith*

His pleasure mirrors in my soul,
Joy unmeasured,
Abandoned to delight,
Imprisoned with hope,
Faith, its own assurance,
Of our smiling God,
Pleased with the bold,
The courageous, the believing,
He comes, bringing rewards with Him,
For the faithful,
The seekers,
The faith men.

oming to God takes faith. We seek God believing He is there. He is listening. In this kind of faith, we find ourselves in His presence, feeling His touch, hearing His voice.

God is a rewarder. When we seek Him we find Him. He Himself is the greatest reward we could ever receive, yet He also has no problem rewarding those who seek Him with all their heart.

Sincerity would rather say, "I need no reward. God is enough." There is some truth in this. However, it would be an insult to anyone who were to bring a gift and we would ignore it. We bless God when we receive the gifts He offers.

Rewards come to diligent seekers. Prayer is not a "one of" moment. It is a lifelong lifestyle when we want to and when we don't, when it's dark and when it's light, when it's good and when it's bad. Diligence relies on discipline more than anything. Discipline is the key to remaining committed to this lifestyle of prayer.

45

Is anyone among you **suffering**?

Let him *pray*.

—*James 5:13*

suffering

suffering

suffering

We seek comfort,
He seeks our attention.
So pain finds us,
So we find God,
Yet we drift aside asking others,
So another round
The mountain we see,
Till it is, we ourselves, me,
Who prays…

When trouble comes, it's time to pray. It's so easy to seek answers from people rather than from God. However, our instinctive response needs to become that when there is trouble, we will pray first, instead of running to the pastor, the doctor, the banker. Make God the first port of call when there's trouble.

In prayer we will find our way through.

James says "anyone"—not just some special group or person, but you and me—is included in this offer! The purpose of the pain is that we become motivated to pray. Too often we ask others to pray. We call for intercessors. We tell others to pray. All this will help. But IF we ourselves fail to pray, then the prayers of others are limited.

We are the ones who are meant to be praying. The purpose of affliction is to arouse the cry of our heart to God. The times of suffering in a person's life can be the sweetest times in their life if they will draw near to God. Our connection with God deepens in suffering more than at any other time. How many times have I heard people say that even though the time of trouble was terrible, it was also the richest time of their life?

A missionary friend named Diana was captured and imprisoned by the Taliban along with seven others in Kabul, Afghanistan in the early part of 2000. They were held for one hundred days in a small cell with appalling conditions. However, when they were released, her story was that she would have been happy to have remained there longer, because they learned to sing and pray at levels like they never had before. If we're suffering, we should be praying.

46

Is anyone among you s i c k ? Let him *call for the*

elders of the church, and let them *pray* over

him, *anointing* him with oil in the name of the Lord. And

the *prayer of faith*

will save the sick, and the Lord will raise him up. And if he has

c o m m i t t e d   s i n s , he will be *forgiven.*

—*James 5:14-15*

*let them
pray*

Why didn't we call?
"Call, and I will answer."
Call for His servants,
Not theirs to initiate, but ours.
The uninvited prayer carries so little power.
Requested prayers, now they're answered.
Call for help.
Let humility usurp pride.
The elders come,
they pray,
they believe,
they anoint,
We're healed.

When we pray for people, we need to pray with faith. James has already told us that the prayer of faith is to be without doubt or double-mindedness. The prayer of faith imparts faith to the sufferer and engages God. The prayer of faith heals the sick.

The power of God is conducted in an atmosphere of faith. It is prevented from having any effect in the atmosphere of doubt.

*S*in is not always to blame for sickness, but if it is, our sins are forgiven when we call on God for mercy. When the leaders of the church pray for us, they are remitting our sins, and thus we are released from sin and its consequences. The word "anyone" infers that sickness was unusual amongst believers; but if it did happen amongst the people, they were to call for their leaders to use their authority in prayer.

Anointing people with oil is powerful in saying that the power of God is present and is bringing real answers to real problems.

47

Confess your trespasses to one another,

and *pray* for one another,

that you may be healed.

—*James 5:16*

No illness withstanding the tincture of this clean stream.
Heaven opened because of open hearts, open fellowship.
High trust, deep love,
Confesses, prays and heals.

*T*ransparency opens heaven. Even the gold of heaven's streets is "clear"! God lives in light. He is light. There is no darkness in Him, not even a shadow! Our prayers rise to their highest effectiveness in a clean atmosphere. We need to bring our trespasses into the light. This is not the task of others. It is our own burden to bring our faults to the open. We humble ourselves when we confess our stumblings.

The open heart prays easily. The closed soul neither gives nor receives the prayers of saints. Praying for one another releases healing streams. This river of God heals sickness of every kind.

48

The **effective**, *fervent* prayer of a righteous man avails much. Elijah was a man with a nature like ours, and he **prayed** *earnestly* that it would not rain; and it did not rain on the land for three years and six months. And he **prayed** *again*, and the heaven gave rain, and the earth produced its fruit.

—*James 5:16–18*

effective,
fervent

Carmel prophet,
Dark and conflicted,
Lonely, afraid,
Mixed burdens,
For a nation he weeps,
For himself the same.
Yet holding a nation's fate in his grip.
He prays, rain ceases.
He prays again, yellow fire creases a blue sky,
Prophets (false), heads fall under his hand.
He prays again.
No ceremony, just groans of a man on the ground.
His small cloud breaks a drought,
And hard Israel returns to God.

The Bible never masks the flaws of its heroes. Even enormous figures of Scripture such as Elijah, who met with Jesus on the holy Mount, struggled with his own fears, depressions, discouragements, jealousies, and resentments; and yet, his prayers prevailed.

Elijah tells us all that no matter how fickle we ourselves may be, no matter how many challenges we personally face, we can still pray prayers that are effective. His prayers were born of passion and faith. He shows us how we should pray. He prayed with fire and strength and fire returned from the hand of God.

He prayed the unrelenting prayer of a faith that would not give up. He prayed until he saw a cloud emerge on the horizon, and though small, he knew it was the beginning of a breakthrough from the drought.

For the earth to do what it is meant to do, it needs water. Without rain, no seeds will ever sprout. We need to pray for the rain to fall on the seeds of the Word that have been planted over the years in the hearts of thousands.

49

Husbands, likewise, **dwell** with them with *understanding*, giving HONOR to the wife, as to the weaker vessel, and as being *heirs together* of the g r a c e of *life*, that your **prayers** may NOT BE HINDERED.

—*1 Peter 3:7*

unhindered prayers

The withholding man,
His prayers withheld.
Give to her, her honor due.
Give to her your understanding,
Your mind, your love,
Share His grace in your hand to give,
And your prayers will fly
Free from the snare.

The husband must:

Dwell with his wife.

Show her understanding.

Give honor to her.

Respect her.

Bring his strength to bear where hers wanes.

Share the blessing of God instead of hoarding it to himself.

Answered prayer hinges on healthy relationships.

*O*ur prayers can be hindered. Daniel 10 tells the story of how Daniel's prayer was hindered by a demon blocking the angel who was bringing the answer. As Daniel continued fasting, the angels of God eventually broke through, delivering a vision of end times into the prophet's soul.

If we nurse resentments against those we are joined with, the hinderer will block answers to prayer. Our prayers are effective because we have harmony in our marriage.

50

For the eyes of the LORD are on the righteous,
And His ears are open to their prayers.
But the face of the LORD is against those who do evil.
—1 Peter 3:12

the righteous

God answers a man,
Not a prayer.
Even wrong prayers,
prayed by a right man,
Find more grace than right prayers from the wrong.
God's vision is fixed upon the righteous,
Seeking to answer their cry.

Blessing falls upon those who live right. It's the law of the world we live in. God has empowered us to live right. As we choose to be "the righteous," we'll enjoy an abundance of blessings over our lives. Answered prayer is included in this abundance. The Lord listens to the prayers of those who live right. But those who don't, He turns against.

Answered prayer is also contingent upon the life of the person praying. A person living in rebellion against God cannot expect that the God they reject is going to listen to (let alone answer) their prayers. If we are to anticipate answers, then our lives need to be righteous before God, not offensive to Him.

We are saved from hell because we receive the free gift of a perfect life, Jesus. His rightness with God gains our entrance to heaven. However, this rightness of life is something we are meant to embrace for our lives.

51

But the **end** of all things *is at hand*; therefore **be serious** and **W A T C H F U L** in your prayers.
—*1 Peter 4:7*

watchful

Eyes open, sleep goes,
Real prayer awakens my soul.
If tomorrow we die,
What matters today?
What things to cease,
What things to begin?
Prayer uncovers,
We recover our eyes.
We see again
What prayerless souls cannot.

*W*e are close to the end of the world. We need to awaken to those things that really matter, becoming "watchful." This awakening to our state and the state of the world around us, comes through prayer. We are "self-aware" through prayer. We "wake-up" when we pray. Without prayer we're blind. Asleep! Without prayer we fail to see any danger in our decisions. In prayer, conviction grips us. If the world were going to end tomorrow, what would we do today? This is Peter's context. "The end of all things is at hand…therefore." This shapes us. We cannot be apathetic in prayer. Unbelievably, most people can't even get themselves to pray, let alone take their prayer life from where it is to a state of urgency.

Be urgent in prayer. The world is about to end!

52

Beloved, I pray that *you may prosper* in all things and be in **health**, just as your *soul prospers.*
—3 *John* 2–3

soul prospers

Love begets wishes and dreams,
Prayers for friends.
Prayer sweetening the friendship,
Heightening our love.
We ask for the simple, the broad.
"Blessing in everything,"
Healing, health, and joy.
Unimaginable that we would pray for disease and poverty,
Yet misguided sincerity,
Parading piety,
Disclaims John, refers to our "real" world.
Harsh teaching presenting harsh God.
Fools. You fail to hallow His name,
Sacred in love, to prosper His family,
Not stay His hand from His children,
Not Him, creator of billions, creatures and color,
He delights to prosper, to bless.
And so we pray His will be done,
For friends, for family.

We should tell people when we are praying for them, and what we are praying for. The power of attorney that we have empowers us to pray for things others feel unable to pray for themselves.

The greatest gift we have for friends is prayer. We should not wait for people to have trouble before we take time to pray for them. If we love people, the best thing we can do is to ask God to bless them. Our prayers for our friends should be generous and full of blessing.

53

But you, *beloved*, building yourselves up
on your most holy faith, *praying*
in the Holy Spirit.

—Jude 1:20

in the spirit

Who will build me? Me!
My life built by prayer,
My faith strong,
Holiness pursuing,
My spirit prays, soaking,
Submerged in Him, Holy Spirit.

Every time we "pray in the Spirit" (most easily interpreted as "praying in tongues"), we strengthen ourselves. Strength comes from prayer. A vast variety of advantages enter our lives through prayer. A person's value to people and their meaning in life is the sum of their commitments. Our commitments harness our potential and focus it on whatever we give ourselves to. When we are committed to prayer, we strengthen ourselves and build our faith.

There are three kinds of supernatural languages ("tongues") the believer can be gifted to speak in:

Other languages they have never learned (see Acts 2).

Angelic languages (which require interpretation; see 1 Corinthians 14:5).

Unknown languages, for, "he who speaks in a tongue does not speak to men but to God, for no one understands him" (see 1 Corinthians 14:2). This is the most commonly used supernatural "tongue" by far. This is a prayer language that exceeds our understanding, which means that we are communicating in the Spirit the yearnings of our soul.

Speaking in tongues strengthens and "tunes" our spirit. God is not a poor communicator. We are often slow in being able to hear what God is saying. However, when we spend our days in prayer, our inner man is attuned to communing with God.

Jude declares that we are strengthening ourselves every time we pray in the Spirit.

54

And the **smoke of the incense**, with the *prayers of the saints*, a s c e n d e d before God from the

angel's hand.

—*Revelation 8:4*

prayers ascending

Sweet scent of the redeemed,
Their voice, their tears,
Their worship, incense for God,
To flavor prayers,
Succoring answers from on high.
What voice my prayer?
What scent my spirit?
Sour hearts corrupting worship,
Silencing prayer's voice in heaven.
Hateful words a stench.
Turning murderous prayers to dust.
We repent.
We give thanks.
We praise.
We worship.
Our prayers rise in incense.

The four living creatures and the twenty-four elders fell down before the Lamb, each having a harp, and golden bowls full of incense, which are the prayers of the saints.
—Revelation 5:8

There are obviously processes in prayer that are beyond our understanding. However, angels are clearly involved in both taking our prayers to God and in bringing back the answers. Genesis 28 tells of how Jacob saw angels ascending and descending the stairway to heaven in his night vision. Judges 13:20 tells of an angel ascending in the flames of the altar to Samson's parents. It was an angel telling Zacharias in Luke 1:13 that his prayers had been heard. And in Revelation 4:10, the twenty-four elders fall down in worship before the Lamb of God, who is holding golden bowls full of incense that are the prayers of saints:

Our prayers are presented to God by intercessors at His throne. Our prayers have an aroma, which indicates the spirit of each prayer we pray. We need to ask ourselves if the aroma of our prayers is pleasing to heaven, or if they carry the stench of this world—selfishness, anger, revenge, greed. Are they scented with brokenness and obedience, faith and praise, surrender and worship? It is a question well worth asking. What does the fragrance of the spirit of your prayers smell like in heaven?

55

Even them I will bring to *My holy mountain*,

And make them *joyful* in My house of prayer.

Their burnt *offerings* and their s a c r i f i c e s

Will be *accepted* on My altar;

For My house shall be called a house of prayer for all nations.

—Isaiah 56:7

house of prayer

Rejection vanquished,
Love including,
None beyond the reach,
This House, this House of Prayer.
All come,
All prayer,
All joyful,
Dizzy with acceptance,
Dancing with God.

The House of God is a House for all nations. There is no nationality, no tribe, no people created on earth prohibited from His House. We are a multinational community. Prayer is common to everyone on earth. Singing and music are different nation to nation, worship styles are different, but prayer is the same wherever we go in the world. All the walls are dismantled and "all nations" can unite in God's House of Prayer. When we find ourselves in different nations, or meeting in multinational communities, we know the one thing that we can do together is to pray.

*I*saiah pushes the prejudice boundaries when he tells the exclusive Jewish community that "even foreigners" will come to their holy mountain to worship their God, and that "He" will be the One who brings them. These foreigners celebrate in the House of Prayer. Their offerings will be acceptable along with Jewish sacrifices.

56

Abraham prayed to God; and God healed Abimelech, his wife, and his female servants. Then they bore children.
—*Genesis 20:17*

he will pray

Unhealed and barren like Sarah,
Sick, diseased and desperate,
Naive Abimelech and his palace.
Uninnocent Abraham,
Yet blessed with a power.
The power of sickness or health,
Life or death,
Barren or fruitful,
Lay in his grasp.
IF He asks, you will live,
IF not...
He asks,
They live.

*T*he background to this story is difficult to come to terms with. Abraham has asked Sarah his wife to say she is his sister so the local king will not kill him and abduct her into his harem. Sarah was a beautiful woman. The king does take Sarah, without killing Abraham, because he is under the impression she is Abraham's sister.[1] However, a plague comes upon the entire kingdom of Abimelech. God speaks to Abimelech, revealing the true state of affairs. Angered, he returns Sarah to Abraham with many gifts. He asks Abraham to pray that the plague stop.

Even though Abraham had behaved badly by lying to the king, his prayers still carried the power to deliver a nation from a plague. This is because Abraham was a covenant man—God had made a covenant with him, making Abraham a prophet and intercessor appointed by God.

Each of us falters and stumbles, but this does not mean we can't pray. It's precisely at these times that we need to come to God. Our prayers are no less effective. It is precisely at these times that we need to come to the Lord boldly asking for mercy and grace to help in our time of need (see Hebrews 4:16).

note
1.   Sarah actually was Abraham's half sister (see Genesis 20:12).

57

Therefore the people came to Moses, and said, "We have sinned, for we have SPOKEN AGAINST THE LORD and against you; *pray* to the LORD that He *take away* the serpents from us." So Moses prayed for the people.
—*Numbers 21:7*

moses prayed

The twang of the whine,
A black magic,
Summons the vipers,
Charms the bite.
So many bitten,
So many dead,
Unconscious of the curse of the complaint,
Now awakened with pain,
Crying for the prophet's prayer.
So he prays.
The asps retreat,
Their poison ink faded
Bloodstreams cleansed,
With a look, with a view,
Of the cross,
Standing high in their wilderness.

The Israelites feel the pain of God's anger. Snakes plague the desert floor, snapping at the Israelites' heels. They repent from their thankless complaining. They come to Moses for help. They confess they have spoken against God and Moses. They ask for prayer.

Prayer is ineffective unless it comes from the heart. Prayer is not a matter of simply chanting a few correct phrases and imagining that will have an impact against a problem. This is mere superstition. Real prayer has its fountain in the heart.

For Moses to be effective, his prayer needed to usher from his heart. These people had been complaining about him and his leadership, accusing him of wrong motives, being cynical about virtually everything he did, and now they are asking Him to pray for them. This is the heart of a great man. He prays and God answers. The heart of Moses was always for the Hebrews, even when they were dark and murderous. This reveals years of preparation in the man of God. He remained meek in the face of their violence. He delivered them from their destructions through his prayers.

58

Then Samson **called to the LORD**, saying,
"O Lord GOD, *remember me*, I pray!
STRENGTHEN ME, I pray, just this once, O
God, that I may with one blow take
vengeance on the Philistines for my two eyes!"
—Judges 16:28

samson called

O Samson!
If only we heard your cry before.
But now, blind anguish,
Tragic heart,
Knowing the promise, but,
Lost, dropped, fallen to the floor,
What could have been,
What was meant to be.
But now in death,
"I will destroy more than in life,"
This is my prayer O God.
If all the "if onlys" could be redeemed.
Ah! Happy day, they can.
The death of One destroyed them all,
And dead dreams rose with Him, to live again.

his is the only recorded prayer of Samson. Had he been a man of prayer, he would not have found himself in this predicament. Praying men don't sin and sinning men don't pray.

Even though Samson was called to deliver Israel from the Philistines as a judge, he never did. When we fail to pray, we will find ourselves drawn into temptation greater than our capacity to resist. Prayer is the antidote to temptation. Every person is tempted and every person can pray. This is the simple answer to prevention in everybody's life. Samson's life purpose was never fulfilled. His compromise destroyed his destiny. He aggravated and troubled the Philistines but never removed their domination over Israel. He is the only judge who did not manage to vanquish the oppressing nation.

Anyone carrying an extraordinary anointing such as Samson's (no one else ever did) must recognize their need to remain in a place of devotion to God. The attraction of the anointing is high and many women want the man carrying that power. But it's like superman. As soon as superman agrees to become fully human so he can have the girl of his dreams, the power that was once so attractive also drains. Every person has their own brand of kryptonite, and playing with it only "disempowers" us and destroys the purpose God has arranged for our lives.

In his dying moments, Samson manages to kill more Philistines than in his entire life. Imagine what he could have accomplished if only he'd had the same level of desperation while he was free to rid the nation of the oppressors! The person who rules his spirit is the person that can deliver a city.

A paper clip was invented with a purpose. We all have a higher value than a paper clip. God invented all of us with distinct purpose. Each of us have a destiny. However, we also encounter situations that intend to totally destroy that purpose.

59

And she was in **b i t t e r n e s s   o f   s o u l** , and *prayed to the LORD* and *wept* in anguish. . . . **And it happened** , as she **continued** *praying* before the LORD, that Eli watched her mouth. Now Hannah s p o k e   i n   h e r   h e a r t ; only her lips moved, but h e r   v o i c e   w a s   n o t   h e a r d . Therefore Eli thought she was drunk. So Eli said to her, "How long will you be drunk? Put your wine away from you!"

—*1 Samuel 1:10, 12–14*

her lips moved

The ache of Hannah,
Too deep for voice,
Yet heard on high,
Misread on earth,
Chided for a prayer,
Exceeding irony,
Samuel is born,
To replace the priest,
And make the kings, of Israel.

ome prayers are too painful to give voice to. Hannah's ache that she had never given birth was exacerbated by her husband Elkanah's other wife, the graceless Peninah, who had borne him several children and constantly taunted Hannah for her fruitlessness. Hannah's husband loved her. He tried to pacify her grief by giving her twice as much as he gave to Peninah. But nothing stopped Hannah's deep ache.

Hannah brings her pain to God. She prays, but the high priest Eli chides her for drunkenness. This man would not chide his two ungodly sons, but he very misguidedly rebukes a godly woman. Eli's discernment had been corrupted. We are told that Eli was obese. Under Eli, the ark was lost from Israel to the Philistines. Eli's problem of lack of discipline was through his personal world and his family.

However, once Hannah explained her plight to him, Eli blessed her. Hannah's prayer was answered and Samuel was born—one of the greatest prophets and leaders in all the history of Israel. He was dedicated into service in the temple under the very same Eli. And Hannah then gave birth to other children as well.

When our motives or prayers are misunderstood, we should not be discouraged. Opposition to prayer comes in many forms, however it should not stop us from seeking God and bringing enormous answers from heaven that can give birth to nation changers, such as Samuel.

60

These all continued with one accord in *prayer and supplication*, with the women and Mary the mother of Jesus, and with His brothers.

—*Acts 1:14*

continuing

To begin, one thing.
Continuing, another.
With "one voice," a miracle!
The recipe, the birth,
His Church is born, in prayer.
Prayer, how long?
As long as it takes!
Who?
Anyone!

*J*esus went to heaven assuring the disciples that they would receive power IF they would pray, waiting in Jerusalem. They got together and kept praying. About five hundred heard the call (see 1 Corinthians 15:6). Maybe they all went to Jerusalem.

Prayer is a humbling exercise. Even Jesus' mother, Mary, included herself amongst the prayerful. She could have (but didn't) excuse herself from the prayer meeting (as is the habit of some who consider themselves important). The angel had declared her blessed above all other women. Other women and the brothers of Jesus were now all praying together. The cultural mores separating the sexes broke in the prayer meeting.

The prayers of men and women ascended together to God.

They were in "one accord," like a symphony of individual instruments together, they composed a beautiful single prayer to God. They had singularity of purpose and mind. They wanted God. They were seeking Him to fulfill His promise of supernatural power. They were committed to simply staying until the promise came. That was the condition Jesus had placed upon them in Acts 1, to "wait" for the promise of God.

If there were five hundred at the beginning, the number had certainly shrunken by the Day of Pentecost, when there were only one hundred and twenty present. But then maybe this is also a natural filtering that persistent prayer has—just as Gideon's army was diminished by selecting those who drank in the manner of soldiers, as compared to those who drank like animals. God purifies His people. He was seeking the chemistry of unity among His disciples. This provided the foundation for the Holy Spirit to fall. And fall He did! The rest is history.

And they continued steadfastly in the apostles' doctrine and fellowship, in the breaking of bread, and in prayers.

—*Acts 2:42*

continuing steadfastly

Prayer, sweet Cinderella,
Oft forgot, easily ignored,
Quickly stirred,
Quicker to fade,
Can grow and die in the same day.
But the steadfast, the true,
They continue, and continue, and continue.

*T*he newly born church committed themselves to just four things. Remember, these people shook the then-known world, creating a movement that continued to gain momentum, right down through the centuries to this very day.

World-shaking churches always own prayer as a foundational work.

Nothing would stop them from praying. Their commitment was sure.

"Prayer is always in place in the house of God. When prayer is a stranger there, then it ceases to be God's house at all. Our Lord put peculiar emphasis upon what the Church was when He cast out the buyers and sellers in the Temple, repeating the words from Isaiah, 'It is written, My house shall be called the house of prayer.' He makes prayer preeminent, that which stands out above all else in the house of God. They, who sidetrack prayer or seek to minify it, and give it a secondary place, pervert the Church of God, and make it something less and other than it is ordained to be. Prayer is perfectly at home in the house of God. It is no stranger, no mere guest; it belongs there. It has a peculiar affinity for the place, and has, moreover, a Divine right there, being set, therein, by Divine appointment and approval." [1]

—Edward M. Bounds

note

1.   Edward M. Bounds, *The Necessity of Prayer* (Bellingham, WA: Logos Research Systems, Inc., 1999).

62

Now Peter and John went up together to the temple at the hour of prayer, the ninth hour.
—*Acts 3:1*

hour of prayer

To go together,
Friends to prayer,
To go each day, at that hour,
That hour of prayer.
Two by two to everywhere.
To preaching, to prayer.
The adventure, the journey,
A path of miracles that changes the world.
Go to prayer!
Stay in prayer,
Leave in prayer.
Who knows the shakings prepared?

We shouldn't imagine that prayer is reserved for just when we are inspired to pray. The early church had set hours of prayer. So should we! These were one hour prayer meetings. Many miracles would occur on these journeys. On this particular time, a lame man was healed at the Gate Beautiful. Peter and John were two of the closest to Jesus, and now their relationship continues in spiritual pursuits. There were moments when their relationship was strained. At one time Peter claimed he would follow Christ when all the others would fail. He had been chided by Christ after His resurrection in front of all the other disciples. Yet now they are bound together in the same purpose and ale to go to the temple and seek God together.

63

And when they had *prayed*, the **place** where they were assembled together was **shaken**; and they were all *filled with the Holy Spirit*, and they **spoke the word** of God with boldness.

—*Acts 4:31*

shaken

Weather from another world,
Shakes ours,
If we touch heaven,
With our prayers,
Bathed in harmony,
Returning in trembling.
Filled with Him,
Not us,
Speaking His word,
Not ours.

They are filled with power after prayer, then they speak the Word with boldness. Prayer, filled, and bold. Prayer is not just about asking God to do things. Immediately after praying, the apostles were filled with the Holy Spirit. Filled with the Spirit, they preached with astonishing authority and confidence.

*T*he end of praying should be the start of something. Prayer should get results.

Here is the pinnacle of "something happening." The whole building shakes as they reach the "Amen" of their prayers. After we have prayed, a presence, a peace, a stirring, a shaking, something, should happen! Real prayer has an immediate impact on the atmosphere. Not only is the climate affected, we are too.

64

But we will give ourselves **continually** to *prayer* and to the *ministry* of **the word**.

—*Acts 6:4*

given to prayer

We all give ourselves.
To what, we choose.
No higher habit
To addict to,
Than prayer,
Than Word.

*I*nternal problems had arisen within the church. Persecution had hit them from without but not from within. This was a first. It was a "racist" problem: Purist Hebrews wanted the Hebraic women to be preferred above the Hellenistic, Greek-speaking women when it came to support from the church. The apostles were approached to come and settle the dispute, but they refused. Their commitment was to the Word of God and prayer, not to administration. They delegated the responsibility to seven men filled with the Spirit, faith and wisdom. The apostles ensured that they would remain true to the basics so the life of the church would not be hindered.

Possibly our greatest problem in today's church is our preference for management instead of prayer. We pray, study, and seek God at the beginning of our ministry, but then growth comes, which demands administration, problem solving, and management. This is when a minister must resist being dragged into the details of the daily operation of such duties. Our primary calling remains our highest calling. What brought growth at the beginning, sustains growth at all times. Our calling is prayer and study. Through this we build the House that endures forever.

65

...whom they set before the apostles; and *when they had prayed,* they laid hands on them.
—*Acts 6:6*

laid their hands
on them

laid their ha
laid their hands
on them

Praying before, not after,
It's first, not last.
Praying, then choosing.
It's the way of the Kingdom.
Seek first,
Then all else after.
Who to choose?
Is not the question.
Have we prayed?

he laying on of hands sets people apart for a calling. It also empowers them with anointing for the job. Gifts are given, revived, and released by the laying on of hands. Without prayer though, this is a meaningless exercise. Effective prayer in the power of the Spirit releases the anointing.

When we pray, we arouse this gift for others to receive.

Impartation is how God empowers us. God places within one what He wants to place in others. When it's time for us to receive a gift, a healing, a miracle, He most often places it in another person who is then meant to impart it to us.

66

So the Lord said to him, "go to the street called Straight, and inquire at the house of Judas for one called Saul of Tarsus, for behold, *he is praying*. And in a **VISION** he has seen a man named Ananias coming in and putting his hand on him, so that he might receive his sight."

—Acts 9:11-12

unceasing prayer

I breathe unceasing,
So I live unending.
I pray unfading,
My spirit breathes heaven.
Some things seasonal,
Some things for a moment,
Not prayer.
She seeks voices
That untiring cry,
Call and seek, asking His will.

When the Holy Spirit falls upon us, prayer is where we go. We become more aware of a spiritual world and less connected with the natural world. When the Spirit comes, so also do visions and dreams.

When he was praying, Paul saw Ananias coming and praying for him and he received his sight. God had also appeared to Ananias in a vision, and told him to seek out Saul. This was precarious because all the believers feared Saul, knowing him as the arch-persecutor of Christians. However, when we pray and when God has spoken to us, our fears are dissolved and we will find ourselves doing things that others may not understand; but because our confidence is based on a real revelation of what God has planted in our heart through prayer, we are bold.

67

But Peter put them all out, and knelt down and prayed.
And turning to the body he said, "Tabitha, arise."
And she opened her eyes, and when
she saw Peter she sat up.

—*Acts 9:40*

knelt down
and prayed

Put them out!
Clear the air!
Fill the room with faith.
Fill the place with prayer!
Pray, don't rush to the answer.
It's a word, a deed, a vision, a sound.
We'll never know unless we pray.
Tabitha cries from the dead,
"Pray. Hear the words that raise me.
Hear the sound that makes me breathe again."
This young, dead people wait for the people of prayer.

*P*eter had been in the room when Jesus raised the daughter of Jairus from the dead. Peter, recalling how (in Mark 5:40) Jesus had put out everyone except a few believers, does the same. His first action is to pray on his knees. After a time he turns and speaks life into the dead. The young girl Tabitha is raised from the dead. Who knows what transpired when Peter prayed?

Many times we are left in the dark regarding how God actually communicated with people throughout the Bible.

We are simply told that God spoke to people (or not even that), yet how people heard or were guided is rarely clear. We are, however, clearly shown the process insomuch as the servant of God prayed before anything at all happened. Peter would have prayed for some time here, until he heard from God. Even the word he spoke would have been planted in his spirit from the Lord while he prayed.

Without prayer we have no access to the wisdom, strategies, and words of God.

68

"YOUR **PRAYERS AND YOUR ALMS** HAVE COME UP FOR A MEMORIAL BEFORE GOD."

—*Acts 10:4*

memorial

God's memory prompted,
How?
Prayers and alms.
Yes, pray as ye give,
Give as ye pray.

Our prayers create a memorial along with our giving before God. God is mindful of us because He hears our voice. His thoughts are towards us because we gain His attention with prayer and fasting. Often Scripture refers to God "remembering." We draw the Lord's attention our way when we seek Him. He draws near to those seeking Him, to those drawing near to Him. Our prayers certainly rise. They "come up" before God. They create a place in heaven for us. They form a place in the memory of God's mind.

He is mindful of those who pray.

69

The next day, as they went on their journey and drew near the city, **Peter went up on the housetop to pray**, about the sixth hour.
—*Acts 10:9*

anywhere prayer

A housetop, a basement,
A park, a mall,
A car, a bus,
In prison, on a mountain,
At school, in bed,
At work, at play,
At midnight,
In the morning,
Noon or eve,
Never a time,
Never a place, where prayer cannot go.
No excuse, no reason.
We can always find that place.
That place to pray.

*B*utterflies have to spread their wings in the morning sunshine because the scales on their wings are actually solar cells. Without that source of energy they cannot fly. Prayer is our source of energy: When we spread our prayers out before God, He endows them with His power and they accomplish His purpose.

Whenever and wherever we are, there is always somewhere we can pray. The person committed to prayer will find a place to pray. If we are committed to prayer, the excuse that there is nowhere for us to retreat to will not be ours. There is *always* somewhere. I am always traveling. Whether on a plane, in a crowded hotel, in a convention, a conference, there is always somewhere to pray if I look for it. I have seen sunrises in a thousand different places around the world, because I simply want to be up before the sun to seek the Lord. Some of the most beautiful scenes I can think of are those early morning prayer walks.

Along icy rivers in St. Petersburg, canals in Amsterdam, the beaches in Sydney, the snowy streets of Tahoe, the heated mists in Fiji, the smoky streets of New York, or the muggy humidity of Bangkok. Every time through the sunrise with my prayers and I have found my place for the day.

Peter goes to a rooftop to pray at the sixth hour and a vision comes to him that reveals God's plan to extend the Kingdom to bringing in the Gentiles. Unless we find a place to pray and unless we actually go to prayer, we will not see the visions God intends for us. How many projects have been left undone simply because we failed to pray? Our need is to find our closet or rooftop, and spend time praying. If we don't, then things cannot be improved.

"If there is no snow in the mountains, there will be a drought in the plains." [1]
—Laurie Beth Jones

note
1.   Laurie Beth Jones, *Jesus CEO* (New York: Hyperion Books, 1995).

70

Peter was therefore kept in prison, but constant prayer was offered **to God for him by the church.**
—*Acts 12:5*

constant prayer

Find your knees for others.
Stay, till doors open.
No prison strong enough,
No castle tall enough,
No law binding enough,
To prevent the prevailing,
The constant,
The church.

The sad thing is, sometimes it takes the imprisonment and persecution of a leader to arouse the church to a new level of prayer. We must realize that souls are imprisoned right now by their own guilt, shame, sins, and demonic biding. As we arise in constant prayer, we will see the power of God release the bound and set them free.

The church didn't approach the government to try and get their leader released. They sought God. Human officials decided to keep Peter in prison, BUT the church prayed—and not just one or two leaders, but the whole church, and they didn't just offer one or two prayers, they prayed constantly. Prayer is not something to be done by the person up at the front all alone. Prayer needs to be something the entire church is engaged in.

71

Then, *having fasted and prayed,*
and laid hands on them, *they sent them away.*

—*Acts 13:3*

prayer sent

Bathed in prayer,
We are sent with power.
With fasting we fuel these prayers with power.
This power, this key.
We need again,
To our knees,
To prevent the impotent,
The wasted sent,
Achieving nothing but that they went.

The early church realized that their power was resident in their fasting and praying. They were not doing this to discover direction, but rather to impart blessing by the laying on of their hands. We need to send and receive people with prayer. In the spirit of prayer, prophecy and guidance comes. It was not just one person fasting. They all prayed. This theme is constant throughout the Book of Acts. The church functions corporately, not singularly.

We have understood "Come," but not so well have we grasped, "Go." As much as we would fast that people would come, we need to fast and pray for people to go, as in the command of Jesus to send out workers into the harvest fields (see Matthew 9:38).

72

So when they had *appointed elders* in every church, and *prayed with fasting*, they commended them to the Lord…

—*Acts 14:23*

prayer appointed

The church built on people,
Naught else.
Destroyed by the same.
Naught else.
Wrong man,
Wrong place;
The seal of doom.
Right man,
Right place;
How, but by prayer?
The "called," offered to God in prayer,
Commended, blessed,
Favored, prevailing.

The appointment of leaders in the church was surrounded with prayer and fasting. They treated the selection and delegation of Christ's authority with great sacredness. Their fasting and prayers commended them into the hands of God.

We commit our ways into the covering of God through prayer. Unless we commit ourselves to God, we are not committed. This commitment is real, not notional. It is acted out in prayer and in fasting.

73)

And on the Sabbath day we went out of the city to the riverside,

where *prayer* was customarily made;

and we sat down and spoke to the women who met there.

—*Acts 16:13*

sabbath prayer

Empty traditions,
Void and abounding,
Filling calendars with nothing.
O for customs fastened to power,
O for the custom of prayer.
If we dismiss all others
And return to this,
We fill the fruitless church,
With power,
With Him.

*P*rayer is a custom of the church that needs reviving regularly. The women gathered at the riverside to pray. Women seem more easily given to pray than men. Our ego doesn't always enjoy the notion of depending upon another, even asking another. Just try getting a man to ask for traffic directions from anyone. "We know where we're going. As if we need to ask anyone!"

Yet, here were a group of women that became the foundation for one of the greatest churches in history. Again, prayer lies at the base of the awesome new moment in the expansion of the House of God.

Prayer prepared the women to hear from the apostle. Once they heard, they recognized this was God and the Philippian church began.

74

Now it happened, as we went to prayer, that a certain slave girl POSSESSED WITH A SPIRIT OF DIVINATION met us, who brought her masters much profit by fortune-telling.
—*Acts 16:16*

deliverance prayer

First this, then that,
Then this, then that.
So much troubling the path to prayer?
Neither people nor things.
But hell's envoy,
Flattering, accusing,
Anything to prevent prayer.
Cast it out!
Clear the way!
Bind the binder!
Set captives free!
Fix your heart.
Nothing will prevent me,
From prayer.

*T*he girl followed them for several days before Paul exorcised the demon from her. The devil will do all he can to aggravate us and distract us from prayer. We will find ourselves under attack as we go to prayer. Yet this very thing can also be the great opportunity we have been looking for if we turn the aggravation to action and begin to bind powers that are invisible, yet causing tangible hindrances.

Whatever is trying to stop us from prayer, we need to bind. There will always be a hundred reasons why not to pray. It is too easy to underestimate the power of prayer. The devil is the greatest opposition to prayer. The sooner we deal with every hindrance to seeking God, the sooner blessing will fall on our lives.

75

But at midnight Paul and Silas were *praying and singing hymns to God*, and the prisoners were listening to them.

—*Acts 16:25*

midnight prayer

Deep and dark,
Dungeon dark,
Bloodied backs
Rattling chains,
Cold, dank, and bound.
What else but sing!
What else but pray!
Loud, loud, louder.
No private religion here,
Prayer's voice rising at midnight,
Crumbling a prison's might,
Freeing the guilty
With the righteous.
How?
Prayer!

Instead of prayer coming up out of worship, we need to lay a foundation of prayer, and let worship arise from that.

They were unashamed of the other hardened criminals listening to their unusual response. We can never let our embarrassment over our worship and adoration and prayers prevent us from giving full vent to all that is in us, even though other people who could easily mock us can hear us.

What would we do at midnight, whipped, bleeding, unknown in a foreign country of a different language, in the deepest darkest dungeon the persecutors could find? Paul and Silas began to pray and sing. This tells us that the tone of their prayers was not solemn. They were faith-filled, joyful songs born of a spirit of prayer.

76

And when he had said these things, he *knelt down and prayed* with them all.

—*Acts 20:36*

departing prayer

Ending, Paul prays.
Ephesus, Diana's domain,
Fallen to Christ,
Through Saul become Paul.
Now your conqueror leaves,
Weeping, praying,
With shepherds of the flock.
No deeper bonds forged,
No closer ties felt,
Than those of prayer.

aul's last words to the Ephesian church leaders were deeply important: "Take heed to yourselves and to all the flock, among which the Holy Spirit has made you overseers" (Acts 20:28). These leaders wept at Paul's departing, mostly because they would no longer hear from him. Yet, beyond all his words, the very last ministry Paul exercises among them is to kneel down and pray with them all. My sense is that the words "prayed with them all" means that he prayed with each one, believing God for them all to fulfill all of the will of God in their lives.

We should pray for all, and also for each. The personalized prayers for one another carry powerful meaning for each individual. At the moment of departure, it would not be hard to imagine that prayer opened the door for Paul to prophesy over each of them as well.

When "fathers" were departing throughout Scripture, often they would bless their children with blessings specific to the individual person. Our prayers should not be restricted to the general. If we bend our ears to heaven, we will hear specific things we are to pray over each person.

77

For **God is my witness**, whom I *serve with my spirit* in the gospel of His Son, that *without ceasing* I make mention of you always *in my prayers*.

—*Romans 1:9*

prayer for those we haven't met yet

The art of one,
Asking for another,
This key of the Kingdom
Building the church
Over there.
Our prayers
Not for us,
But for them,
Those we've never seen.
Those we always see,
In prayer.

*P*aul had not yet been to Rome, yet he ceaselessly prayed for them. Some of the most important writings in the New Testament are contained in the letter of Paul to the Romans. This letter was born out of prayer for people he had yet to meet, but as he prays, revelation pours out toward them. His references at the end of the letter show his love for all those he does know in Rome.

Eventually Paul does arrive in the Emperor's city, from where he writes many epistles to the churches around the world. This entire journey of high accomplishments began because he prayed continuously for people he knew he was destined to minister to, yet hadn't ever met. We need to pray for those people we are about to meet, the places we are going to, the work we are going to do. Our praying will open doors for us and reveal things to us we would never think of in our natural mind.

...rejoicing in hope, patient in tribulation, continuing steadfastly in prayer.

—*Romans 12:12*

always prayer

Hope landed,
Troubles arrived,
Both reasons to pause,
But neither really.
The pledge to pray,
Survives the day,
Whether bright or dark,
Rich or poor.
Steadfast,
We continue.

*L*ife in God has moments that are wonderful, but that is not the walk He has called us to. The Christian life is a steadfast walk. It is not just one prayer that will take us into victory. It is steadfast, unrelenting, persistent prayer. If we keep ourselves in a consistent prayer life, we will find ourselves also enjoying a consistently joyful life. We will find ourselves with patience in times of trouble. Patience is length of spirit. Our spirit gains patience and strength through praying. Our stamina in prayer increases as we pray more often. The reason we are unable to sustain spiritual activity is that our stamina in that area is not high. It is precisely the same as the physical: When we exercise, our stamina for more exercise increases. Our prayer "muscles" increase as we continue steadfast in prayer.

79

Now I beg you, brethren, through the **LORD JESUS CHRIST**, and through *the love* of the Spirit, that you **strive together** with me in prayers to God for me.
—*Romans 15:30*

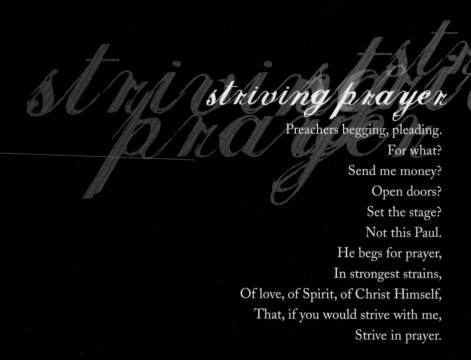

striving prayer

Preachers begging, pleading.
For what?
Send me money?
Open doors?
Set the stage?
Not this Paul.
He begs for prayer,
In strongest strains,
Of love, of Spirit, of Christ Himself,
That, if you would strive with me,
Strive in prayer.

Paul "begs" the Romans, not for money, opportunity, help or workers, but for prayers. His greatest need was for others to fight with him in prayer.

All leaders in the church should seek the prayers of their people. This fact on its own creates a bond between leaders and followers in addition to the strengthening power released by their prayers.

After Paul has written his lengthy letter to the Romans, he pleads with them through Jesus and the love of the Spirit that they enter into warring together in the Spirit in prayer for him. To "strive together" is to enter into severe effort with another. Paul was continually in a war against the powers of darkness. He regularly urges all those to whom he writes to pray for him. His burden was not small.

Pray for your leaders, your pastors, your associates. Fight for them in prayer. Resist the devil off of them. Bind Satan from attacking them. Stand before God for them. Argue for their blessing.

80

Do not **DEPRIVE** one another except with consent for a time, that you *may give yourselves* to fasting and prayer.

—*1 Corinthians 7:5*

sacrificial prayer

So many couples failing,
Young love dying,
Faint commitment flagging,
Thinking sex is the savior,
The reason, the maintainer,
The all in all of love.
Last days gone mad.
Cease, for a moment,
Come aside and pray,
Cease from food, for a moment,
Come aside.
Higher appetites thirst and hunger.
We satisfy,
With God.

David humbled himself through fasting (see Psalm 35:13).

The door to the Gentiles was opened through the fasting and praying of Peter (see Acts 10).

In the 1 Corinthians 7:5 passage, Paul is advising married couples to enjoy sex, but to abstain during times of fasting so they can devote themselves to prayer and fasting and, rather than feed their carnal appetite at any level, feed their spiritual life through a total commitment to prayer.

asting and praying engages the highest-octane spiritual power available. Fasting has always been a practice of effective believers.

Jesus began His ministry with a forty-day fast.

Moses birthed the Israel nation by ascending Mt. Sinai and fasting in the presence of God for forty days.

Paul began his ministry after he was saved by fasting for three days (see Acts 9:9). He declared he was in "fastings" often.

Nehemiah fasted with the burden of Jerusalem upon him (see Nehemiah 1:4).

Ezra fasted with the burden of the people's sins (see Ezra 9:5).

Daniel fasted to receive a revelation God wanted to impart (see Daniel 9:3).

Fasting covers the whole concept of ceasing to satisfy the cravings of our flesh. This self-denial allows our spirit to rise. We become clearer and sharper. Spiritual qualities surface where they had been dormant. Always satisfying our flesh dampens the quality of our spiritual life. Creating space for our spirit takes us to new levels. Our prayers increase in effectiveness when fasting is added.

We need to "pray" the price for others to be saved, healed, and set free. We give our lives for others when we fast and pray for them.

81

But *every woman* who prays or prophesies…

—*1 Corinthians 11:5*

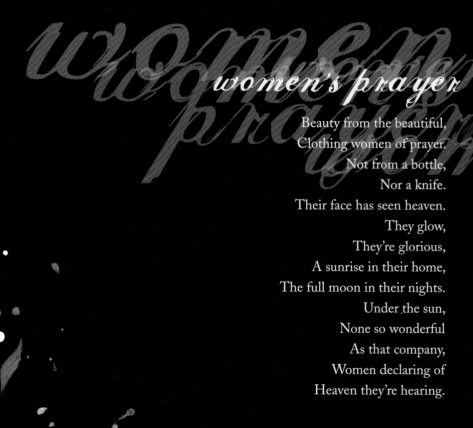

women's prayer

Beauty from the beautiful,
Clothing women of prayer.
Not from a bottle,
Nor a knife.
Their face has seen heaven.
They glow,
They're glorious,
A sunrise in their home,
The full moon in their nights.
Under the sun,
None so wonderful
As that company,
Women declaring of
Heaven they're hearing.

western culture, wearing a hat or not carries little significance. We need to do those things that send the signal clearly that we are following the basics of Scriptural guidelines. Foot washing, for example, is not a practice among us and is not necessary to carry on as a regular practice; however, it is *serving one another* that is the central message. Doing those things normally reserved for a hired help to do is what we are called to do for one another.

or some reason women generally have been the greater people of prayer than men have been. When Paul tells Timothy in 1 Timothy 2:8 to tell the men everywhere to lift up holy hands in prayer, it seems as though he doesn't need to tell the women. Firstly, women are more easily given to prayer than men. Secondly, many women tend to have far less ego to deal with, so the lifting of hands (or any spiritual expression, it seems) is generally far less challenging to them than men.

When we pray under authority, we pray with authority. The person who is without submission to anyone is also without any authority. We will all find moments when we need to submit to authority against our better judgment. None of us will know whether we are submitted or not until we are doing what is difficult for us.

Over the centuries and still to this day, endless discussions rage over the question of whether women should be allowed to minister or carry authority in the church. Here Paul is saying that they are definitely to both pray and prophesy. As with anyone though, they are to exhibit that they are under the authority of the local leader. However, in our

82

Therefore let him who speaks in a tongue pray that he may **interpret**. For if *I pray in a tongue*, my *Spirit prays*, but my **understanding** is *unfruitful*. What is the conclusion then? I will pray with the spirit, and I will also pray with the **understanding**.

—*1 Corinthians 14:13-15*

interpreting prayer

This doorway in my spirit,
This language,
Unhinging my mind,
From here to there,
Sharpening my spirit,
Tuning my soul,
Awakening the interpreter,
My spirit, the candle of God.

*A*s we saw in chapter 43, there are three different kinds of "speaking in tongues." Two kinds are *messages* that are spoken; the third kind is *prayer*.

The first is what happened on the Day of Pentecost. Supernaturally they spoke in other languages they had never learned.

The second is above when we speak out a message in an angelic language that no one understands unless it is interpreted. When someone does this, they are to also pray for the interpretation, so they can shift from speaking in tongues to speaking in the local language. When we pray in tongues, our spirit prays.

The third is "unknown tongues" which "no man understands. However he speaks mysteries to God."

When we speak in tongues, our spirit is activated. Speaking in tongues is the least of the gifts, which is great because it allows us access into the supernatural zone at the simplest and easiest level. All of us can become people who move in the Spirit, simply by speaking in tongues. Whatever God has placed in our spirit will surface when we speak in tongues.

Paul says we need to pray both with our understanding and with our spirit, so we are praying intelligently and spiritually.

...praying always with all prayer and supplication in the Spirit, being watchful to this end with all perseverance and supplication for all the saints; and for me, that utterance may be given to me, that I may open my mouth boldly to make known the *mystery of the gospel.*
—*Ephesians 6:18–19*

praying in the spirit

Pray when?
Always, never not.
With what?
All prayer, all of it.
How?
In power,
The Holy Spirit of heaven.
For whom?
All saints, not one left out.
And for me.
For what?
That my fears are drowned in faith.
That boldness opens my mouth,
With the message,
That delivers from hell,
Gifting access to God.

The biggest exhortation to prayer in the New Testament is right here, with Paul calling on us to pray always with all prayer and supplication in the Spirit.

There is a great variety of prayer, which means we can constantly be in prayer. All prayer needs to be in the Spirit, meaning we are to throw ourselves into the exercise. We intercede, we give thanks, we rebuke, we resist demons and darkness, we command, we confess, we proclaim, we profess, we groan, we supplicate, we glorify, we praise, we wait, we worship, we quiet our soul, we rise shouting against hell and against devils and enemies threatening those we love. Prayer is prophesying, asking, seeking, receiving, believing, communing, watching. All of this connects us at every level in every way with God Himself.

84

Be **anxious** for **nothing**, but in everything by prayer and supplication, with *thanksgiving*, let your requests be made known to God; 7 and the *peace* of God, which surpasses all **understanding**, will guard your *hearts* and minds through Christ Jesus.
—*Philippians 4:6-7*

unburdening prayer

Dark anxiety,
Dancing with our minds.
We unhand you with prayer,
Casting all of you on God.
Peace you sit us down,
Displacing depression,
You fortress our troubled minds,
And hearts uneasy.
Prayer stands guard each day,
Withstanding worry's assault
Healing bruised minds,
Keeping peace within our walls.

*W*hat an amazing command. "Don't worry!" About anything! Instead, pray with faith about everything and you'll enjoy unassailable peace. Worry comes uninvited. We need to respond to this anxiety with prayer and faith. Every day there is something to be anxious about. Sometimes anxiety comes for no reason at all, shivering through our soul, upending every security we have. The antidote to anxiety is prayer "with thanksgiving." Prayer may not always do it. *A worried prayer ain't no account.* There are times when prayer on its own can be just another form of worry. But when we pray with thanksgiving, we are saying thanks for the past, thanks for the present, thanks for the future, and thanks for answering our prayer. Even though we have no evidence of our prayer being answered, we have *the promise of God* telling us that the prayer of faith is answered. This is evidence enough—even more than what we can see with our eyes.

We must learn how to transfer what we are worried about over into the hands of God. Prayer is how we "cast our burdens" on the Lord. Once we have prayed, even though we feel anxiety wanting to consume us again, we refuse it any place in our emotions, put our mind on other things, and leave it with God.

Anxiety is at the root of depression, which is epidemic in societies around the world today—even leading to death in many cases. Not being anxious is not just a nice thing to do, it is *imperative* for our well-being. Once we have entered into a faith with God over whatever is overwhelming us, the peace of God—which is more powerful than anything we face—will literally guard our emotions and mind from mental illnesses.

Don't worry about it! Pray about it! Believe that your prayer is heard, and leave the problem in God's hands.

85

Continue **earnestly** in prayer,
being **vigilant** in it with **thanksgiving**.

—*Colossians 4:2*

vigilant prayer

Thankful hearts,
Forgotten too easily in life,
Remembered easily in prayer.
Gratitude revive in me,
Complete the circle of blessing.
From Him to me, from me to Him.
Prayer if only for this, is enough.
To bring thanks,
To bring praise.
To remember all He's done—
And will do.

*P*rayer is not something we do only in a moment. Like breathing, prayer is a continuing exercise throughout our life. It is meant to be *ongoing*. We keep praying no matter what attempts to hinder us from it.

It's also meant to be earnest. We do it from the heart. There are dangers we need to be awake to. Prayer alerts us to threats we would otherwise be unaware of. Our watchtower is prayer. We gain a higher perspective and can see further.

Thanksgiving is the atmosphere of effective prayer. We would be foolish to underestimate thanksgiving. Thanksgiving is the doorway into the presence of God. It is humility to be thankful, because it declares that God is the Source of our success. Thankfulness disarms criticism and complaining. Giving thanks enhances any experience in life because it includes another's joy. How many times have you celebrated a moment and wished a friend was there to enjoy it as well? Thankfulness to God brings Him into the experience. Tuning our mind towards thankfulness forces us to think of positive things and to see the positive in negative circumstances. Appreciation for all of life is bundled into thankfulness.

86

Epaphras, who is one of you, a **bondservant** of Christ, greets you, *always* **laboring fervently** for you in PRAYERS , that you may *stand perfect and complete* in all the will of God.

—*Colossians 4:12*

laboring prayer

I say I serve You,
Then I pray.
I labor with fire,
I labor in prayer,
Not for me, but for them,
My people, my town,
My family, my friends,
That they stand,
And standing they obey
You, O God.

The prayers of Epaphras were not problem-oriented, but rather purpose-driven. He wanted them to be complete in the will of God. Just because a thing may be the will of God, does not necessarily mean it will happen. We pray His will into being. Even Jesus recognized this when he instructed us to pray, "Thy will be done" (see Matthew 6:10 and Luke 11:2).

*P*rayer is work. Real prayer cannot be carried out in a halfhearted, distracted way. Real prayer is exacting. Most believers can't pray for long because the stamina, strength and fitness of their spirit cannot sustain any length of time in the work of prayer.

The Colossian Epaphras was on fire in prayer for his home church. Our success in our churches depends on praying for them. If God has planted us in a particular family, we need to pray for them.

…night and day PRAYING
exceedingly that we may see
your face and perfect what is
lacking in your faith?

—1 Thessalonians 3:10

night and day prayer

Overburdened
Overwhelmed
Prayers to match desire
To see You
To complete You
To build You
To inject our faith
In You.

hen we cannot be physically present to do what must be done, we can pray. Paul prayed "exceedingly" that he would be able to visit the Thessalonians and complete whatever they lacked in God. We all know people we feel could do with help, yet too often we rush in where angels fear to tread. We should pray before we see people and try to correct them or try to bring something to them we feel they are lacking.

Once people are born again, they need to keep moving forward. If they stagnate, chances are they'll wither. We need to keep praying for people after they have been saved with the same intensity as we did for them to get them saved.

88

Therefore I exhort first of all that supplications, prayers, intercessions, and giving of thanks be made for all men, for kings and all who are in authority, that we may lead a quiet and peaceable life in all godliness and reverence. For this is GOOD AND ACCEPTABLE in the sight of God our Savior, who desires all men to be saved and to come to the knowledge of the truth.

—*1 Timothy 2:1-4*

first prayers

Before all others,
Prayer,
For all men,
Prayer
That all men
Might be saved.

*P*rayer is the "first of all." It is not a last resort. Prayer is the priority call for every believer. It should be the first action on our daily schedule. It needs to be the first action in any decision-making process. It should be first, as in before, we do anything in a number of steps. It should be considered the most important thing we can engage in.

Paul is not referring to polite, respectable praying here, the kind that is offered as a somewhat perfunctory requirement that lacks heart and authenticity. The Apostle includes intercession in the list of the kind of prayers to be offered. This is the deepest most ardent prayer form and cannot be exercised without obvious energy. We must provide ourselves with environments in which we can "work" in prayer without holding back because of fear of being seen as unusual. I don't think we should be "unusual" in inappropriate settings. We need a "closet" into which we can hide and seek God without reservation.

Paul also calls on us to "give thanks for all men." We are to flavor our prayers with grace, faith, and forgiveness. No matter what people we can think of—from the worst to the best—we are to give thanks for them. Giving thanks changes our perception of everybody and everything. We cannot give thanks alongside unforgiveness; so thanksgiving "air-conditions" our soul, blowing out stale, heated air.

When we give thanks for "all men," we are believing for a result different to their current situation. We are seeing them following Christ, praying, reading the Bible, in fellowship, worshipping in church, fulfilling their ministry.

89

I desire therefore that *the men pray everywhere*, lifting up holy hands, without wrath and doubting.

—*1 Timothy 2:8*

men's prayers

O for men of prayer,
Leave it not to the ladies.
Egos low, la femme praying easily.
An apostle's desire.
The cry of his soul,
That men everywhere
Pray everywhere
Losing their rage,
Laying down their doubts,
They lift holy hands
Across the land.

The hands they lift are to be set apart to God for Him, not engaged in false dealing with money or in signing documents that are wrong. Their hands are to be holy from the world of sex and uncleanness. Hands that have helped and hugged, hands that have healed and reached out, hands that have given generously and supported the weak.

aul had a vision for men to pray. *Men need to pray.* But their pride too often prevents them—something that can be overcome through praying.

They are to lose their angers, resolve offenses, forgive everyone for anything ever done to them, absent doubt from their mind and heart, and choose to believe the things that they are praying *will* come to pass.

They are to pray everywhere, at work, home, and at church.

They are told to lift up their hands. The women need little encouragement for this, but men tend to be reticent at overt spiritual expression.

90

For **EVERY** creature of God *is good*,
and **NOTHING** is to be **REFUSED** if it is
received with thanksgiving; for it is
sanctified by the word of God and *prayer*.

—*1 Timothy 4:4-5*

sanctifying prayers

Pray over it all.
Your days, your nights,
Your ins, your outs,
Your ups, your downs,
Your work, your play,
Your parents, your children,
Your food, your stuff,
Set it apart,
Bring it under blessing,
Under the hand of God.

Paul tells Timothy that nothing is to be refused if it is received with thanksgiving and prayer. The strict food laws of Judaism prevented them from eating anything unapproved by the laws of Moses. Only certain foods were "set apart" for the Jewish people. However, New Testament liberty sets us free from such laws.

When we pray over something and consecrate it to God, it becomes blessed to us. Praying over a meal with thanksgiving before we eat is a rich Christian heritage. There is also the sense that if there is any problem with the food that we are ignorant of, prayer will solve that. We should pray over everything we are "receiving" into our lives so that it becomes a blessing to us, and that if there are problems with it, they will get solved. Pray over people you are receiving into your world in relationships, over new clients, new opportunities. When we invoke the hand of God upon our world, we can expect His blessing on what we do.

Even within the Christian world we have a heritage that has built up artificial and unnecessary laws whereby we imagine that God requires them if we are to remain in right relationship with Him. But here we discover that "nothing is to be refused if it is received with prayer."

…who, in the days of His flesh, when He had offered up prayers and supplications, with vehement cries and tears to Him who was able to save Him from death, and was heard because of His godly fear.

—*Hebrews 5:7*

Jesus' prayers

Jesus prayed,
Who am I to think
Beyond prayer I am.
The beloved Son,
The only One,
Crying, lurching toward the cross,
Tears, bloody sweat,
Yet no complaint,
But worship, surrendered and strong.
Listened to from on high.
Raised from the dead,
Answering Gethsemane's prayer.

hy does God hear our prayers? Our attitude! Jesus reverently submitted to the will of God. He poured out his entire soul in loud cries and many tears. Supplications (*hiketeria* in Greek) literally means carrying an olive branch wrapped in white wool and bands as we approach for help. It is coming with surrender to the One from Whom we are seeking help. He was heard by God because of his "reverent submission" to the will of God in a supplication that doesn't complain, but rather cries out to God, not in anger but in appeal. Our willing obedience to the will of God opens heaven and God hears us.

Obedience, it seems, is not intrinsic to any of us. Even Jesus learned obedience. The way we "learn" obedience is that when we reap the consequences of disobedience, we realize that it is much better to become obedient in life, rather than rebellious.

Even though Jesus had prayed the most desperate prayer of His life and was "heard," it is easy to imagine He was not heard. After Gethsemane, He suffered more than any man—and then was crucified and entombed. From all appearances, it would seem that His prayers were completely ignored. However, it is obvious that Jesus eventually emerged victorious.

Just because we have been heard doesn't mean there is an instant change in our circumstances. Change often takes time. In fact, the things we are seeking deliverance from can sometimes get worse before they get better. We shouldn't judge the effectiveness of our prayers through immediate visual results. We need to remain in a state of faith, believing that God has heard and that the wheels are turning that will bring the change we seek.

92

Then Jesus came with them to a place called Gethsemane, and said to the disciples, "SIT HERE while I go and *pray* over there." And He took with Him Peter and the two sons of Zebedee, and He began to be s o r r o w f u l and *deeply distressed*. Then He said to them, "My soul is exceedingly sorrowful, even to death. STAY HERE and *watch with Me*."
—Matthew 26:36-38

watch with me

No deeper bond forged,
No more intimate time than now,
In the pangs of death
My soul cries for friends.
To talk with? No.
Just be with me, as I pray.
Pray with me in my pain
This sadness too deep
I'm drowning but for friends,
Friends with me who pray.

esus invites the three disciples into the most intimate moment of his life. As he enters prayer, He feels sorrow and distress. In fact, when He felt even greater agony He prayed more earnestly (see Luke 22:44).

When we feel distress, sorrow, agony, these are times to pray with even greater intensity. If Jesus felt the need to pray in His times of agony, how much more do we need to do the same?

93

When all the people were baptized, it came to pass that Jesus also was baptized; and **while He prayed**, the *heaven was opened.*

—*Luke 3:21*

he prayed

Heaven closed,
So easily opened,
Opened by a prayer.

When we pray, there is every reason to expect an open heaven. As we pray—especially in obedience to God—the greatest opening of all is made available to us. We live under an open heaven. Jesus has given us His name. Praying in His name is as if He were praying Himself.

Supernatural experiences happen "while" we pray. These can be quiet and easily unnoticed, but as we sensitize ourselves to the movings of the Spirit, we become aware of God's movings within us.

94

Now in the morning, having risen a long while before daylight, He went out and departed to a solitary place; and there He *prayed*.

—*Mark 1:35*

early prayer

Early, alone,
In the dark,
In the night,
I've got to get away,
I've got to pray.
There I can talk,
There I can cry,
There I can sing undistracted,
And worship my God.
I've got to find time,
Time enough to pray,
'Til I connect with the Spirit again.

Charles Spurgeon spoke of a fellow minister: "*Mr. Joseph Alleine, he did rise constantly at or before four of the clock, and would be much troubled if he heard smiths or other craftsmen at their trades before he was at communion with GOD; saying to me often, 'How this noise shames me. Does not my Master deserve more than theirs?' From four till eight he spent in prayer, holy contemplation, and singing psalms, in which he much delighted and did daily practice alone, as well as in the family.*"[1]

*I*n 1985 a minister spoke in our church on prayer. He told me he rose at 5:30 every morning for prayer. I didn't believe him, but he assured me it was true. At the end of his meeting he invited us to his altar call for prayer. He laid hands on me. Since that time I have risen at 5:30 most every morning for the last 21 years, sometime earlier. I believe that simple habit has been enormous as a key to virtually every area of blessing I have experienced in my life. There are days when I would pray for up to three hours, but mostly it's around one or two hours a day. And this is not praying while I'm doing work or walking around church—that should be norm in our lives.

If I am wanting to serve God effectively as a minister, there is no way I can expect to do that without a solid prayer life. If Jesus, the Son of God, felt the need to withdraw to pray before the sun rose, who do I think I am to not need that? It's obvious to me the disciples recognized that His secret was prayer, thus they asked Him to teach them how to do it effectively.

note
1. Charles H. Spurgeon, *Lectures to My Students on the Art of Preaching* (London: Marshall, Morgan and Scott, 1954).

95

So He Himself often w i t h d r e w into the wilderness and *prayed.*

—*Luke 5:16*

praying alone

"He's aloof."
"Where'd he go?"
"Unsociable."
His society is heaven,
His companion, God.
His needs few,
His prayers abundant.
The wilderness a palace
For the king of prayer.
We follow him from the noise,
To the wilderness.
Our palace, too, of prayer.

*W*illiam Wilberforce, the political crusader who brought an end to Britain's slave trade, lamented his busyness:

"This perpetual hurry of business and company ruins me in soul if not in body. More solitude and earlier hours! I suspect I have been allotting habitually too little time to religious exercises, as private devotion and religious meditation, Scripture-reading, etc. Hence I am lean and cold and hard. I had better allot two hours or an hour and a half daily. I have been keeping too late hours, and hence have had but a hurried half hour in a morning to myself. Surely the experience of all good men confirms the proposition that without a due measure of private devotions the soul will grow lean. But all may be done through prayer—almighty prayer, I am ready to say—and why not? For that it is almighty is only through the gracious ordination of the God of love and truth. O then, pray, pray, pray!"

To pray is difficult, because it means getting away from those things that present themselves as urgent, important, essential. To withdraw is to extricate and disentangle ourselves from the pull of a thousand and one legitimate claims on our time and energy. We must decide well before the moment that we are going to get away and pray—at all costs. It means we have to face God. It means we are going to be alone, which for some personality types is tortuous. But to pray effectively, we need to withdraw. To have a relationship with God, we have to spend time alone with Him.

Is He precious to us or not? Do we value a relationship with God or not? Would we rather be doing something else or be with someone else or not? Jesus did not want to be with His Father only occasionally, but often. It was in the wilderness, the same place where He had beaten the devil, that He found time with His Father.

96

And when He had sent the multitudes away, He went

UP ON THE MOUNTAIN by Himself *to pray*.

Now when evening came, He was alone there.

—*Matthew 14:23*

prayers on a mountain

"To the mountain," our spirit cries,
"Climb higher,
Where no others go."
Alone, alone, but unlonely,
Wet with anointing,
Drenched with Hermon's dew.
Laughing in frozen air,
His joy, mine.

Everyone wanted Jesus, but He sent them away because He wanted God more than fame or adoration of the crowd. More than being needed, He felt that He was the one who was in need. He wanted to be with His Father. Whether it meant withdrawing into the wilderness or climbing a mountain, Jesus ached for God. He was alone but not lonely. He made time with God in the evening and in the morning.

A preacher who claims he is too busy to pray needs to look at the One he claims to serve, the One who didn't find time but made time, by sending away those things that encroached upon His chosen moments and threatened to intrude into His most essential practice: prayer.

97

Now it came to pass in those days that **He went out to the mountain to pray**, and continued *all night* in **prayer to God**. And when it was day, He called His disciples to Himself.

—*Luke 6:12-13*

all night

Forgive us Lord,
You sought all night,
Then chose Your twelve.
Whenever have we done this?
We choose too early, too late,
We choose by our eyes,
We choose by our ears,
By those who refer,
And never by prayer.
Before we choose,
We choose to pray,
And Lord those men,
This world will sway.

efore selecting those disciples who were to become apostles of Christ and thus the foundation of the church, Jesus spent the entire night in prayer. Choosing the right people is the most crucial task in building the church. We can so easily be deceived by our natural inclinations or by our so-called "experienced eye." However, if we would spend a night in prayer before we select people for crucial positions, then we would make far fewer mistakes. Before we appoint people, we need to pray and feel clarity and peace. The right delegation will leave an enduring legacy. The wrong delegation destroys good history.

...*casting* all your care upon Him,

for He cares for you.

—*1 Peter 5:7*

unloading care

He cares, He cares, He cares.
For you, for me.
Why can't we believe it?
Throw anxiety away,
Throw it to Him.
He'll take it all,
He'll work it out,
Because He cares.

All of us feel anxious about something at some time. There is not one thing we need to carry as a burden. If we are a leader, we will carry burdens every day. As a pastor, I am burdened every day about someone in our church or in the 200 other churches I also oversee around the world.

Those burdens are generally from God. They feel like "care." The line between "care" and anxiety is very fine. If I don't cast my cares upon the Lord, it will morph into depression. Casting cares upon God means that I pray them out to him until I sense a release, and then I leave them with Him; and every time I am tempted to begin worrying about them again, I simply refuse to.

The foundation of belief that enables us to cast cares upon God is that He cares for us. We must believe this and know that He is unprepared for us to carry around anxieties that would destroy us if they remain in our emotions.

99

You will *make your prayer to Him*,

He will hear you,

And you will pay your vows.

You will also declare a thing,

And it will be **established** for you;

So *light will shine* on your ways.

—*Job 22:27-28*

declare!

Acquainted with Him
Through prayer
Abandons requests to answers,
Makes my mouth a power
Unreckoned with,
nature bowing,
Light brewing
For this heard man.

We establish God as the first priority in our life when we dismantle all other things that steal our attention and affection from Him. He will not share our hearts with any other, and neither should we. When He is first, our prayers are heard. This is obvious because those prayers will reflect His purposes (not ours) as the priority. Our purposes become subservient to His.

Prayer is not always about asking. Prayer includes declaring. There are many things God has told us to do simply through declaration, yet we persist in asking Him to do them. Paul even says it is unnecessary for us to ascend into heaven to bring Christ into a situation. He says the Word is in our mouth, so that IF we speak it, we will find ourselves moving the mountain. Jesus told us to *speak to* the mountain. This is not praying to God so He will move the mountain. It is speaking *to* the mountain.

Many times we are told to speak to inanimate things and anticipate that there will be a change. The key factor is in the fact that we believe that what we say *will* come to pass.

100

Therefore **submit to God**. RESIST the devil
and he will F L E E from you.
—*James 4:7*

submit, resist

Sovereign will of man,
Unrealized power.
Till you resist the resister.
Tell it to go.
Shout it loud.
The giant retreats,
Diminished and small,
Bound and fettered,
Chained in prison,
Your power now known:
You rule.

Even though we may consider the Word of God, the blood of Jesus, the Holy Spirit, and the Presence of God the most powerful forces in this world, they are powerless if our will is not aligned with God's. God has made us sovereign in the earth. This means our will rules. If we do not resist the devil, he remains entrenched. However, once we set our wills against Satan, we will be victorious through the power of the name and blood of Jesus.

For us to discover the power of God, we need to be submitted to His will. We only discover if we are, when we are challenged with something that is contrary to our direction. Obedience is never seen until we have to do something we don't want to. Our authority over the devil is based on the fact the God has authority over us. We have submitted ourselves to Him.

We are in a war. We need to be delivered from evil on a daily basis. We should resist the devil from around us, on us, and even in us, whenever necessary. Just like we need to clean ourselves daily, so we need to cleanse ourselves from spiritual defilement regularly.

Prayer is our time for cleansing and purifying.

101

Draw near to God and *He will draw near to you.*

—*James 4:8*

draw near

Unbelievable invitation,
The ultimate intention,
To be near,
To be close.
He draws and draws and draws.
I seek and seek and seek.
My God You are there,
We meet.

mongst the giants of promise in the Bible, this one stands out as one of the greatest. If our hearts ache for God and we separate ourselves to seek Him, He will not hide from us nor make Himself difficult to find.

We draw near to God when we draw away from distractions. Closeness to God takes time and focus. It happens neither casually nor quickly. We draw near to God alone, in quiet, with the door closed on everything else but Him. Prayer is the environment, not the goal. We are drawing near to God, not to prayer. God does draw near to those who draw near to Him. He is not afar off. He is not a principle or a "force." He is a Person, and He responds to anyone seeking to commune with Him.

102

However, this kind D O E S   N O T   G O out

except by *prayer* and fasting.

—*Matthew 17:21*

deliverance

What? Rid evil by wishing?
It calls for prayer.
And fasting too!
Violence demands violence;
Ours greater than evil.
Extract the poison,
The asp, the fly,
Remove the shadows,
With power from high,
Authority gained in prayer and fast,
We eject dark powers,
Free at last.

We are called to deliver people from demon power. Without fasting and prayer at the foundation of our ministry we are laughable to the devil. Seven sons of Sceva tried to be powerful with the name of Jesus, but without a relationship with Him they were stripped naked, overpowered, and themselves cast out, instead of them accomplishing the opposite. Does the devil know you? That particular demon declared that it knew Jesus and Paul, but asked, "who are you?"

We need to gain power over the devil in the Spirit through fasting and prayer. We are called to bind the strong man (see Matthew 12:29 and Mark 3:27). The tools in our hands are prayer and fasting. There is a price to effectiveness. We are guilty of inventing a vast plethora of impotent substitutes for the power of the Spirit. The reality is that we will be effective in the world of the Spirit through employing spiritual tools which include—at the top of the list—fasting and prayer.

103

Then I will *pour out a spirit of grace* and **prayer** on the family of David and on all the people of Jerusalem.

—*Zechariah 12:10, NLT*

spirit of prayer

Spirit of prayer,
Fall on us we pray,
Till we find ourselves praying,
Ceaselessly,
Through all our days.
Credit, we claim none,
You alone are our source,
Gifted to pray,
Gifted to call,
This gift we seek,
This gift we claim.

God has promised to arouse prayer in His people by not just sprinkling us, but by pouring out the spirit of prayer upon us. The grace of prayer enables us to do what we find difficult to do ourselves. When the spirit of something is poured over us, we love that particular thing and give ourselves to it. We become motivated and empowered by the Spirit to pray. We become anointed to pray. If we give ourselves to prayer, it will flow easily and pleasurably. The greatest joy in this world comes from the presence of the Lord when we pray.

Prayer is where Jesus is uncovered to us. We realize our responsibilities in His death. We mourn. Our emotions become tied to our spirit. Prayer is the place of encounter.

104

Let us therefore come **boldly** to *the throne of grace*, that we may obtain *mercy* and **find** *grace* to help in time of need.

—*Hebrews 4:16*

pray bold

Fearless when fearful,
So sorry, so pained,
Disappointed, dismayed,
Myself failed again,
Yet not discouraged,
To come to Him,
To the throne,
To mercy,
Receiving grace,
A witness within,
All is all right.
His mercy prevails.
We hear the herald,
Bell ringing,
Marching heaven's paths,
"The blood of Jesus prevails,
The blood prevails."

e need mercy when we've done wrong. When we're guilty of wrong, to come boldly to God, the Judge of all, is a high call. Yet the exhortation stands: "Come boldly." This is how we will find grace. Boldness contacts grace. The Lord invites us to present our case in such a way that we may be declared righteous (see Isaiah 43:26). The call to come boldly is in light of the fact that Jesus has felt all the weaknesses and flaws of life in the flesh just as we do. Knowing that He understands our predicament, we can come boldly with repentant hearts, knowing we have forgiveness as a covenant right (see Ephesians 1:7). Our need is enabling power, which is exactly what grace provides. Boldness is the key that unlocks all the enabling power of God that we need.

Cowering and groveling to God will neither impress nor move Him. Faith and courage move God. Even when we have fallen short, faith still pleases Him.

105

For the **WEAPONS** of our WARFARE are not carnal but **mighty** in God for pulling down strongholds.

—*2 Corinthians 10:4*

warfare prayer

Weapons dormant apart from prayer,
Powerful beyond belief in the same.
Mighty to defeat the grip, the hold
Of darkness,
Of fears,
Of fantasies,
Of wounds.
Unrelenting
Until
Prayer and weapons
Arrive, unleashed.

him, he gave the invitation once again. This time more than 15 people sprang out of their seats and actually came running to the front to receive Christ as their Savior and Lord!"

The real battle for effective evangelism is a spiritual battle.

*P*eter Wagner relates how a young preacher in South America gained victory in his evangelism:

"*Alberto preached an evangelistic message and gave the invitation. No response! He prayed a strong warfare prayer and directly rebuked the spirits as he had seen Carlos Annacondia do so many times. When he had bound the spirits with the authority that Jesus Christ had given*

106

Call to Me, and **I will answer you**, and show you **GREAT AND MIGHTY** things, which you do not know.

—*Jeremiah 33:3*

call, answer, show

Flick the switch,
Find the Spirit,
Step over the threshold,
Abandon to God,
Lose yourself to Him.
Flow like a river,
Burn like a fire,
Give voice to the burden,
Let it arise.

When we pray, our mind opens to thoughts previously hidden. We are incapable of comprehending those things which can only be revealed in prayer. Without prayer, we remain ignorant of secrets essential to our success for God.

God answers us when we call. He will not mock our praying. He will answer our cry to him—if we will cry.

Jeremiah says God "shows" these things. The Lord communicates through visions, dreams and pictures, using our ability to "see" within our mind, our imagination.

There are great things and mighty things yet to take place in the earth and in our life that no one is yet aware of. Those who cry out to God will discover those things. He reveals His secrets to those who seek Him.

...those who seek the LORD understand all.
—Proverbs 28:5

Moses took his tent and pitched it outside the camp, far from the camp, and called it the tabernacle of meeting. And it came to pass that everyone who sought the LORD went out to the tabernacle of meeting which was outside the camp.

—*Exodus 33:7*

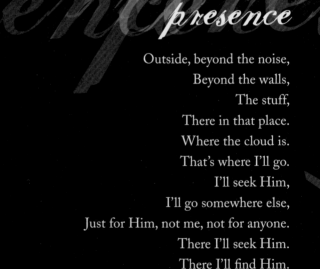

presence

Outside, beyond the noise,
Beyond the walls,
The stuff,
There in that place.
Where the cloud is.
That's where I'll go.
I'll seek Him,
I'll go somewhere else,
Just for Him, not me, not for anyone.
There I'll seek Him.
There I'll find Him.

We should organize a place we can go to where we can meet with God. It needs to be separate from our normal life, "out of the camp."

If the leader seeks God, so will the people. If he creates a space to seek God for himself, the people will also use that space to seek the Lord for themselves. When the leader places a high value on seeking the Lord, so will the people. We need to establish the House of God as a place where people can seek the Lord, where they can pray, not just sing and be spoken to. The House of God must be a place where the people can seek their God.

Moses used his own resources to set up a place to seek the Lord. If the leader will make personal sacrifices to seek the Lord, others will give freely when it comes time to build a permanent structure.

Anyone seeking the Lord had to pass by thousands of other tents and journey out beyond in view of all the tribes. This was at once challenging for a people who were not given to seeking God, and it was also inspiring for those who were double-minded to step out and publicly declare that they would be counted among those who also sought the Lord.

The cloud of the presence descended on the tent when Moses entered. Prayer is not just about us saying things to God. Prayer is entering a cloud, entering a presence, and encountering the living God in a powerful connection every time. Prayer becomes the most exciting event we are invited into with God. In a world with a thousand distractions from movies to computers to books to "going out" to traveling to the never ending fascination with technology and gadgets, it becomes imperative that we make the time and space to encounter God regularly. If we do not make the time and the space, we will never connect with God, because it takes time and a certain undistracted place to achieve unique encounters with God.

But from there **YOU WILL SEEK THE LORD** your God, and *you will find Him* if you **SEEK** Him with all your *heart* and with all your *soul*.

—*Deuteronomy 4:29*

all your heart and soul

Where is He?
Where does He dwell?
At the end of a whole heart,
In the room of an entire soul.
Hidden from the half heart,
Elusive to the casual soul,
Uncaptured by the so-so,
This Lord, jealous of love,
Unsharing your affections.
No matter where I am I will find Him,
With my whole heart.

No matter where we are, or what condition we're in, or what our relationship with God is like, if we will begin to seek Him with all our heart, we will find Him.

This is not just a matter of seeking salvation, healing or deliverance, but of seeking God Himself and seeking to enter and maintain a relationship with Him.

*M*oses tells the people that they can discover the Lord no matter where on earth they are, what condition they are in, or even why they are where they are. In the context of the people being scattered throughout the nations, due to their infidelity to God and being under His punishments, Moses tells them that they will be able to connect with God IF they seek Him with all their heart and soul. This means that when we purify our hearts to seek God with a singular soul, and having a heart for no other loves above Him, then we will find Him. God will not be discovered by the half-hearted nor the shared heart. He is jealous for our first and our best.

...Let the *hearts* of those rejoice who seek the LORD! Seek the LORD and His strength; Seek His face *evermore*!

—*1 Chronicles 16:10-11*

strength from prayer

This bubbling river
Giggling within,
Makes me jump,
Leap and dance,
How could it be,
Those seeking God would be sad,
Those committed, joyless?
Never.
His Presence is joy herself.
Religion, you banal animal,
Go home in your shrouds,
Your misery, your dismal signals,
Spreading joyless death everywhere.
Hallowed be the name of the joyful God,
The only One.

He declares three purposes of the tent and seeking the Lord:

The first is the heartfelt joy that seekers of God own.

*T*his is the Psalm David wrote after he had erected his tent for the ark of the Presence of God. Both Moses and David erected a tent for meeting with God. This is the primary purpose of a church building, a place to meet with God.

The second is the strength we need, which comes from the Lord we seek.

The third is that we discover the face of God when we seek Him. Whatever face we are viewing becomes reflected in our own. We also gain understanding of God's attitude through seeing His face. The opportunity for a face-to-face encounter forever comes to those who are planted in the House of God.

Now SET YOUR *heart* and your *soul* to s e e k THE LORD YOUR GOD. Therefore **arise** and **build the sanctuary** of the LORD God, to bring the ark of the covenant of the LORD and the holy articles of God **into the house that is to be built for the name of the LORD**.

—*1 Chronicles 22:19*

commit to seek and build

Seekers build,
Seeking to build a place for seekers to seek,
For seekers to build,
So build that place,
For a world lost from God,
To return and seek Him.
Seeking they will find.

$\mathcal{S}$eeking God and building His house go hand in hand. God-seekers build the House of God. Those who don't, don't. David and Moses were both serious seekers of God. Both built tabernacles for God to have a "place" to dwell amongst us on earth.

David told the nation to turn their hearts towards seeking the Lord. People who seek the Lord find the desire to build a place where God can dwell.

Whether it's building the people into being the House of God themselves, or erecting buildings that are to be a place for God and His people, it is those who seek the Lord who bring this about.

The primary reason David was exhorting the people to build the house for God was to provide a place for the ark, which essentially was the Presence of God; and when housed properly, treated with reverence, praise and worship, the Shekinah of Moses' time would descend. The presence of the Lord is the indication that He is pleased to dwell among His people, yet He does this because they have set their heart and soul to seek after Him.

And after the Levites left, those from all the tribes
of Israel, such as *set their heart to*
SEEK THE LORD God of Israel,
came to Jerusalem to sacrifice to the LORD God of
their fathers.

—*2 Chronicles 11:16*

sacrifice

O Israel,
Your God, Jehovah,
Is the God,
The great and glorious God of the whole earth.
It is He that made heaven and earth.
All others, pretenders.
So travel from anywhere and everywhere,
To seek Him, to find Him.

Part of seeking God is coming with a sacrifice, an offering with which to bless the Lord.

*J*eroboam disengaged the Levitical Priests, uprooting them from their lands and passing on the duties and privileges to his own appointed priesthood. The Levites therefore made their pilgrimage to Jerusalem to pursue their calling there.

While these people trekked South to worship at the temple, little did they realize this provided a strength for Rehoboam's kingdom so that as the people and he sought the Lord, he maintained the kingdom for the next three years in strength.

The faithful in the northern kingdom also made the journey to Jerusalem at least once a year to bring sacrifices to the Lord, as a protest against their new leader's idolatrous campaign.

This shows us that when leaders show the way, people who hunger for God are emboldened to do the same, to seek the Lord, no matter how far we need to travel, no matter how great the sacrifice has to be.

112

And **HE DID EVIL**, because he did not prepare his heart to seek the LORD.

—*2 Chronicles 12:14*

unprepared

The seeker sins not,
The sinner seeks not.
Hearts changed, purified, holy,
Strengthened, guided,
Protected, arranged with right love,
Passionate for Him.
Evil displaced with good.
Devils replaced with God.
By our choice, our choosing.

our flesh, our environment, our surrounding spiritual atmospheres, and even our relationships. The ability to prevent evil gaining ascendancy over us is the fact that we seek the Lord.

The first step in seeking the Lord is to prepare for it. If we fail to set aside time, arrange a place to seek the Lord, it will not happen. The responsibility to prepare our lives to seek the Lord is upon us, and no one else.

*T*his is the tragic equation in Rehoboam's life, king of Judah, son of Solomon. People do evil when they do not seek the Lord. Even those who do seek the Lord have enough trouble refraining from temptation—how much more those who do not even bother to connect with God for the power to live victoriously. Evil is constantly present with all of us, within

113

Asa did what was good and right in the eyes of the LORD his God, for he removed the altars of the foreign gods and the high places, and broke down the sacred pillars and cut down the wooden images. He commanded Judah to S E E K the LORD God of their fathers.

—*2 Chronicles 14:2-4*

leadership prayer

Courage in a king
Like the sun rising,
Warms cold lands
Brightening clouded days,
Asa turns dark faces to the past,
Removes the loves of idols,
Altars no more.
Just one, for the Lord.
Now nation, seek the Lord,
Unhindered, free.

*A*sa is one of the greatest leaders in biblical history. He reverses the trend of evil kings who have been leading the nation into evil and away from God. Not only does he accomplish a turnaround in his time, but the leaders that come after him are inspired by his example to live for God as well. He removed everything that was obstructing the people from connecting with God. Success in seeking God is dependant as much upon removing negative things from our lives as it is in arranging time for the practice.

Whatever things are in our lives that steal us from time with God, we need to be ruthless with so we are free to seek the Lord. Asa even removed his own grandmother from her position of power as queen mother because she had set up a repulsive idol in the land (see 2 Chronicles 15:16).

Our capacity to do what is good and right depends on the fact that we remove those things from our lives that draw us away from God, and implement those things that draw us near to Him.

114

Therefore he said to Judah, "LET US BUILD these cities and make walls around them, and towers, gates, and bars, while the land is yet before us, because we have SOUGHT THE LORD OUR GOD; we have SOUGHT HIM, and *He has given us rest on every side*." So they BUILT AND PROSPERED.

—*2 Chronicles 14:7*

prayer and peace

Seeking in secret,
Rewards fall public;
Seeking inside,
Reaping outside,
Peace, rest, and the time to build.
Ah yes, seekers prosper, they build.

Asa recognized that God had given them peace because they had sought the Lord, and so he set to work at building cities with great defenses. Both "peace" and "building" come to those who seek the Lord. In fact, those who do not pray are often pulling down what God is trying to build up. God-seekers are builders; those who are not, are not.

We must recognize our times also. When we have peace and blessing, we shouldn't see it as the opportunity to take a holiday. It's time to build. There will always be seasons of war, seasons when we are under attack, or seasons when we need to expand our borders. The greatest walls we can build are the walls of prayer. The greatest towers are those of prayer. The gates and bars we build are firstly spiritual, and are built through prayer. Those who pray will be defended by God Himself. He will be their walls, their gates, bars, and towers. We invoke our best defense when we pray.

...but when in their trouble they **turned** to **the LORD God** of Israel, and s o u g h t Him, He was found by them.

—*2 Chronicles 15:4*

in trouble, in prayer

Trouble, my friend,
My mentor,
Colleague and teacher,
Pounding my door,
Opening me more than any other.
Though I did not seek, now I do.
Though I did not find Him, now I have.
Thank You, Lord, for the pain that raises my voice,
To You.

We must understand that the purpose of trouble in our lives is that God is trying to get our attention. We will cry out to God from places in us we could never tap without the pressure of a trial. Our troubles are designed to turn us to God, not away from Him. We find God when we seek Him, even if it is prompted by problems we ourselves have caused.

If we have trouble today, it's time to seek the Lord. In prayer we see the roots of the problem. In prayer we find the strength to deal with the problem. In prayer we see the answer. We know what to do.

116

Now the LORD was with Jehoshaphat, because he **walked** in the former ways of his father David; he did not seek the Baals, but **sought the God of his father**.

—2 Chronicles 17:3-4

walking in prayer

Ah the leader's power,
We show the way,
Others see and do,
They hear and cry same,
We inspire, we shame,
We require, we command,
Jehoshaphat, smart man,
Does what David did,
Not others.
Finds God.
Finds victory.

There is always some other thing we could seek after, and this calls on us to make the decision that we will instead seek the Lord, rather than collapse towards temptations arranged to destroy our lives.

*D*avid had set out a way of life that would be followed by many other great leaders. David sought God because he loved Him. This became Jehoshaphat's lifestyle as well. The result is that God is with the king. He enjoys prosperity and success throughout most every area and time of his reign. God is with him not because of his personality or because of heritage, position or education, but because *he sought the Lord*. He sought God instead of seeking those things that would satisfy his flesh, in the seeking of the Baals as other kings in surrounding nations were doing.

117)

And Jehoshaphat **feared**, and s e t h i m s e l f t o
s e e k the LORD , and **PROCLAIMED** a fast
throughout all Judah. So Judah gathered together to a s k
h e l p f r o m t h e L O R D; and from all the cities of
Judah t h e y c a m e t o s e e k t h e L O R D.

—*2 Chronicles 20:3-4*

coming to pray

The leader's fears chill his bones,
Crown resting uneasy on a troubled mind,
This one chooses prayer.
His cries fill the temple.
The people gather from Judah's corners,
To cry with their king,
To his king, Yahweh.
Heard from on high,
Victory comes easy,
Prayer, never.

Out of this united prayer and fasting, Judah experienced a miraculous victory over their enemies—through a strategy that no one would have envisioned as being in any way a military reason for success. The choir was sent into battle first, praising and thanking God. The Lord sent hailstones and a great storm into the face of the enemy army, which was innumerable and made the army of Judah appear as a small flock of goats in comparison. They gained victory that day because they sought the Lord.

ear is meant to motivate us to seek God, not to run from the danger, or to seek out help from people, or to simply surrender to the problem. This king had implemented a lifestyle of seeking God; thus, whenever a problem arose, his instinctive reaction was to seek the Lord.

The king called on his entire nation to fast and seek the Lord. A move of God spread through the nation, and people came from every city to the temple to fast and seek the Lord. Because the leader had set himself to seek the Lord, the people followed. This is the incredible influence of leaders. When we pray, we inspire others to pray. When we fast, we inspire others to fast.

118

When You said, *"Seek My face,"*
My heart said to You, *"Your face,
LORD, I will seek."*

—*Psalm 27:8*

my heart said, seek

Oh sweet Scripture,
Is there a sweeter?
Your voice came.
I heard, I sought You.
For nothing but You.
Your face, not Your hand.
Oh Lord, to only seek You would suffice.
But to find You,
To be found of You,
This is my all, yes, my all.

here will be times when we feel
the pull of God on our heart to step
aside and seek Him. We need to have
a regular life of prayer whether we feel
like praying or not; and there will be
times of extended prayer, or special
prayer that the Spirit calls us to.

Our flesh never enjoys obeying God,
but if we will overcome our flesh and do
that thing it so resists—"seeking God
when He calls"—then we will discover
the awesome purposes He has in store
for us.

David felt God pulling on his heart to
seek Him. David responded not with
unwilling, grudging obedience, but from
his heart. His heart loved God. He saw
the invitation as an opportunity meet
again with the Lord.

God calls on us to seek Him, not for
anything else but for Him. God seeks us
to seek just Him, His face (rather than
His hand).

Let's seek the Lord not for what He can
do for us, but for Him Himself. God is
enough. If we had nothing else in the
world, Jesus is more than enough. Out
of Him spring all the elements of the
greatest of lives.

119

I **DID NOT SAY** to the seed of Jacob,
"Seek Me in vain." I, the LORD,
SPEAK RIGHTEOUSNESS, I **declare**
things that are right.

—*Isaiah 45:19*

prayer: never in vain

What?
Seek God in vain?
Could it ever be?
Not a second wasted in His presence.
Not a single moment futile.

It's not in vain God that has told us to seek Him. Our greatest achievements will be because we seek the Lord. He rewards those who seek Him with answers and much, much more. It isn't futile to seek the Lord—even though there may be times when we feel we are not getting many answers for our efforts. We are not alone in this. Even the greatest of Bible heroes felt the same at times. However, there always comes a day when our prayers receive answers and all our seeking pays off.

When God tells us to do something, it is because there is high purpose and awesome results are planned for us.

120

Now My *eyes* will be OPEN and My *ears* attentive to *prayer made in this place*. For now I have chosen and sanctified this house, that My name may be there forever; and My eyes and *My heart* will be there perpetually.

—*2 Chronicles 7:15-16*

this place of prayer

Your house, Lord,
My house, my home.
Here I find you.
In Your house,
Where You live
Here You draw near,
amongst Your people,
Like no other place.
This house, Your house,
Is my house, my home.

he House of God is only that because He is present. If He is not present, it is not in reality the House of God. God lives among His people when they seek Him. This is the foundation for the House of God (not singing nor preaching). These are the fruit of a people and leaders and ministers who are connected to God with the roots of prayer and the Word in their lives.

Prayer is the lifeline of the church with heaven.

The church is meant to be heaven on earth. The atmosphere of heaven should be felt in the church, because she is breathing the air of that place. We are like people walking the ocean floor, hundreds of meters below the surface. Our only hope of life is that we breathe through the pipe connecting us with the surface air. The church's oxygen is the air of heaven. We breathe that air when we pray. The scent of heaven fills the House. The place we have gathered becomes the House of God.

"The life, power and glory of the Church is prayer. The life of its members is dependent on prayer and the presence of God is secured and retained by prayer. The very place is made sacred by its ministry. Without it, the Church is lifeless and powerless. Without it, even the building, itself, is nothing, more or other, than any other structure. Prayer converts even the bricks, and mortar, and lumber, into a sanctuary, a holy of holies, where the Shekinah dwells. It separates it, in spirit and in purpose from all other edifices. Prayer gives a peculiar sacredness to the building, sanctifies it, sets it apart for God, conserves it from all common and mundane affairs." [1]
—Edward M. Bounds

note

1.   Edward M. Bounds, *The Necessity of Prayer* (Bellingham, WA: Logos Research Systems, Inc., 1999).

...but we will *give* ourselves **continually** to prayer and to the *ministry of the word*.

—*Acts 6:4*

habit of prayer

Given or driven,
Pushed or pulled,
Burning or burnt,
All rests upon this life of prayer.
Distractions dismissed,
Hearts bolder than conscience,
Giving task away,
To become Mary, not Martha.
Seeking, Waiting, calling
On You, Lord.
This is our truth, our place.
The church dead,
Led by leaders not praying,
The church alive,
Her servants seeking.

very minister must have a "but" in their life that prevents them from doing those things that distract them from their primary calling, which is "prayer and the Word." There will always be a thousand demands upon our time, attention and energy, but we must be able to say no in order to "give ourselves" to prayer.

Prayer calls for entire "giveness." This cannot be achieved while we are drinking coffee, talking with friends, watching television, working on a computer, reading a book. *Proper prayer is total devotion to the matter*. Many people have a short attention span and become distracted after just a few minutes. Many do not have the spiritual stamina to last more than a few moments in the prayer. Many lack the simple discipline to remain in victory over their own flesh's competition for expression. Effective prayer is "giving ourselves."

The apostles were not just seeing this as a temporary revival measure. They saw it as a lifestyle for the rest of their days. They began a habit of prayer that endured until their passing. They arranged their life so they would "continually" give themselves to prayer and the Word.

They had been approached to assist in caring for the poor widows of the congregation who were being treated unjustly. This in itself is a good work, but it could be carried out by other people just as well. However, prayer and the Word had been committed unto their ministry, and this was not to be the burden of everyone. They therefore delegated the management of the church affairs to others, and ensured that the life of the church was receiving attention at its roots through their prayer and Word life.

Too many pastors and leaders of congregations are actually working as deacons and managers. We must release the ministers to do the work they are called to. And we as leaders must own the courage to fulfill a life of prayer and the Word.

122

As they *ministered* to the Lord and f a s t e d ,
the Holy Spirit said, "Now separate to Me Barnabas
and Saul for the *work to which I have
called them*." Then, having f a s t e d and
prayed, and laid hands on them, they
sent them away.

—Acts 13:2-3

sent in prayer

Called to what?
To ministry.
To whom?
To Him.
First calling, before all else,
We worship, give thanks,
Wait on Him and pray.
From here true men emerge,
Sent from connect,
Sent with presence,
Right timing,
Right men,
Right place,
Right message.
O please pray,
Dear church.
Don't go till you've waited.
The barren Upper Room waits,
For those who would wait.